ROOM FOR PROFIT

MAKE AIRBNB AND THE SHORT RENT REVOLUTION WORK FOR YOU

BY GAYLE ROBERTS AND TRISTAN RUTHERFORD

ABOUT THE AUTHORS

Gayle Roberts was a six year post-qualified lawyer who left the British rat race to start a short term rental agency in 2006. Over a decade later, Pebbles is one of France's leading property letting firms with 180 hotel-style apartments under management. Gayle juggles 20 staff across offices in the UK and France as well as the needs of her two young sons. Her company has won several accolades including easyJet founder Stelios Haji-Ioannou's Entrepreneur of the Year and the *Daily Telegraph* Best of British Accommodation award.

Tristan Rutherford is a multiple award winning journalist who regularly contributes to *The Times*, *The Guardian* and the *Daily Telegraph*. In a previous life he co-founded a property company for the second home market which funded the purchase of his first short term property rental. Tristan has travelled to over 60 countries as diverse as Iran and Belarus, and interviewed property owners in several dozen. His writing has also appeared in the *South China Morning Post* and *The Atlantic Monthly*.

Gayle Roberts and Tristan Rutherford have asserted their right to be identified as the authors of this book. No part of this publication may be reproduced or transmitted in any form without their express permission in writing. The opinions they express are solely those of the original authors and other contributors, and may differ from other peoples' opinions. The contents of this book concentrate on a lightning fast industry and facts described may change. Nonetheless we've tried our best to be accurate and factually correct, but if you feel something is flawed please contact us and we'll consider changes. Just as you should seek a doctor's advice before embarking on any health plan, consult lawyers, financial advisors or at least a few friends before embarking on any new business venture. Good luck.

ABOUT THE AUTHORS _____ 2

Chapter 1: The tale of the garden shed _____ 5

Chapter 2: The money pot and the new poor_____ 9

Chapter 3: The market blossoms on a thousand branches _____ 21

Chapter 4: Making your property short rental ready _____ 25

Chapter 5: A carefully staged photo shoot speaks a thousand
words _____ 41

Chapter 6: Make your rental listing work doubly hard _____ 45

Chapter 7: Expertly honing your asset _____ 71

Chapter 8: Smart but simple money multipliers_____ 74

Chapter 9: The reviews that went wrong _____ 92

Chapter 10: Why your reviews need to go right_____ 95

Chapter 11: When reviews become the market _____ 112

Chapter 12: The longer you rent, the more you earn _____ 116

Chapter 13: I fought the law and the law won _____ 127

Chapter 14: Fifty shades of legal grey _____ 131

Chapter 15: Maximising revenue becomes automated _____ 147

Chapter 16: Onwards and upwards _____ 151

Chapter 1: The tale of the garden shed

"We're just normal people but we make money while we sleep."

"Life started getting good when I started making money."
Balthazar Getty

"To be honest 2015 was a tough year," says Julie Grover. Julie's husband Clive, a freelance oil rig diver, was stuck at home.

When the oil price is high, Clive Grover is flown out to rigs in Nigeria, the Caribbean and further afield. When the price of Brent Crude plummets to $50 a barrel, as it did in 2015, the Grover family are buffeted by the winds of globalisation. Julie took a job in her local Waitrose supermarket in the British Midlands to make ends meet.

"We weren't on the breadline or anything," remembers Julie. "But we have a £650 (€800, $850) a month mortgage on our house and one daughter still at home." An extra £300 a month would make a big difference.

An idea came from Julie's brother-in-law who rents a wooden chalet in his garden near Brighton on Britain's southern coast. "He calls it a log cabin but it's a shed really," says Julie. This self-contained space rents for around £60 per night.

"So if he rented it all week, that would be £400. And if he did that all year it would be £20,000. Of course there are running costs and whatnot but that sort of money is a salary. It gets you thinking."

Julie thought about the spare room her daughter, now a student at Manchester University, had vacated the year before. It was a former office room by the front door of their house with a bathroom directly next door. She pondered redecoration, extra storage, even the price of a new Ikea rug. Late one night a plan formed in Julie's mind.

"I couldn't sleep actually. You know when silly fantasies keep you awake? Well that was me".

Sometime near dawn Julie reached for the calculator on her Samsung telephone. Now, if she could rent the spare room for £20 a night that would be £140 a week. Two weeks of that each month and her money problems were solved.

But what if she could rent it for longer, and for more?

Airbnb, the world's largest short term rental listings website, was fired up on Julie's laptop before breakfast. Her town had a mere handful of single rooms for rent for around £35 per night. The local budget hotels, Travelodge and Premier Inn, routinely charged double that. "I was tingling all over. I'm not a businesswoman but there was a gap in the market."

It took a day of redecoration and a day of fiddling around on the computer to get the spare room listed on a property website. "It was very easy but I only type with one finger so it's not the fastest."

After her listing went live she joined the ranks of over 2.3 million people worldwide who advertise their property for short term lets for free using Airbnb.

In 2016 Julie estimates she earned about £7,000 just from letting out her daughter's room. That's after Airbnb's 3% fee and the price of a new kettle, bags of tea and various cleaning products.

Is she not embarrassed to host strangers in her house? "Well, for £7,000 a year (€8,500 or $9,000) you can take it or leave it, can't you?" Julie says it's like having lodgers in the old days. But you receive a message on your phone with a photo of the person who has booked your place, plus reviews of them from previous hosts. And, most importantly, details of how much money that guest had already paid on their credit card.

The Grover family property empire doesn't end there. As their other daughter leaves home in summer 2017 they've put the entire house on Airbnb for six weeks. "It's when all the festivals and tourists and weddings come to town. Middle-sized houses like ours rent for £130 a night. So nearly £1,000 a week."

Tidying their personal stuff into the attic will be a "pain in the arse". But Julie says she will leave out most of photos, books and *objets d'art* to make her place look "like a warm English home".

Julie's aim is to net £13,000 from Airbnb in 2017. What does that mean to her? "A thousand pounds extra a month is the world. It's a pension isn't it? We're just normal people but we make money while we sleep."

Chapter 2: The money pot and the new poor

"In order to afford the things to which we're all accustomed, we have to think outside the box. The rhythm of school-work-retirement isn't so simple anymore."

"The measure of intelligence is the ability to change."
Albert Einstein

This book will tell you how to emulate Julie Grover. Plus a variety of other short term rental hosts, some of whom earn tens if not hundreds of thousands per year from their properties. We'll talk about Airbnb, rental law and how the accommodation economy will look in 2018. But first we're going to take you on a ten-minute journey through the strange economy we live in today.

Our story starts almost a century ago. During the Great Depression, the Great Depression, the American Economic Review coined the phrase 'the new poor'. This new 'class' of people had the motivation and education to work themselves out of poverty. But lacked the means and opportunity to plough a new furrow.

The Great Depression lasted nearly a decade. It was the first truly worldwide financial crisis. To protect home industry the United States raised import tariffs. This affected the export of Brazilian rubber to America. Which meant that poorer Brazilian rubber makers purchased less French wine. Which meant that poorer French wine makers purchased less American cars. And so on and so forth until, in the three years following the Wall Street Crash of 1929, global GDP had fallen by 15%.

From 1929 to 1933 total exports from Latin America to the United States fell from $1.2 billion to $335 million. American unemployment topped out at 25%. The scene was mirrored across the globe. Think bank runs in Greece, revolution in Thailand and economic catastrophe – followed by a rise in nationalist politics – in Europe.

Sound familiar?

Alas, our leaders have learnt very little. The cause of our current financial crisis is the same as the Great Depression. Before the Wall Street Crash, American brokerage firms could lend $9 for every $1 on deposit. When the market fell, investors called in their loans. Credit was crunched. The entire debt-fuelled economy came crashing down.

We still live in tumultuous times.

For a brief period a few decades later things were easier. The British baby boom generation (born post war between 1946 and 1964) enjoyed free education and gold-plated pensions. House prices routinely cost three times their salary. A growing population increased tax receipts.

Now circumstances are moving where they were a century ago. The gap between rich and poor is increasing, not decreasing.

The 'new normal' of now sees an average house in London costing nine times the average salary. The age of the average first time property buyer is 32. Across 28 European countries the percentage of people aged 18-30 living with parents has risen to 48%. Just 30 years ago Britain had 300,000 people aged over 90. Now it hosts nearly a million. By 2050, one quarter of the UK population will be over 65, with all the accompanying pension costs.

From retirement to education costs it's the same story everywhere. In the US the average medical student will graduate with over $200,000 of debt.

As populations age, government spending must fall. As living costs rise, so real income – the spending power of the money in your pocket – declines.

'The new poor' are not delineated by colour, nationality or faith. In this interconnected world a Ukrainian kitchen fitter can find work in Germany, while a Guatemalan computer programmer may be employed in Canada. Being part of this new global class means that a university-educated graphic designer might earn less than a migrant plumber. Or that your child might not be able to afford the holidays that you once enjoyed.

Of course, people on every income level are pummeled by these winds of global change.

For the rich a declining real income may herald the unaffordability of items taken for granted for generations, like private education or a nanny for the kids.

As currencies slide and interest rates dip, middle income families cut back on foreign holidays. Rainy day funds are replaced by credit cards.

For lower income classes it's tougher still. Drinks after work or cinema tickets become targets for rationalisation – treat items easily replaced with cans of beer or a downloaded movie.

In order to afford the things to which we're all accustomed, we have to think outside the box. Because the regular rhythm of school-work-retirement isn't so simple anymore.

1) La Vita Bella, or life outside the box

Recession hit Italy provides a metaphor to the economy we now live in.

Compared to the advent of Europe's 2008 financial crisis, Italian GDP is less now than it was then. Italians are poorer, not richer, than they were a decade ago. Since then no serious structural changes have been made Italy's banking, corporate or governmental structure. Not one.

Italians used to view a skiing trip in the Dolomites as a yearly treat. It was within their purchasing power. Now a ski week is a luxury only available to holidaying Germans and Austrians spending the same Euro currency.

Until 1992 Italian female government employees could retire after 15 years of service on a full pension. Men could retire after 20 years of government work; 25 years for those employed by local municipalities. This created a mass of pensioners in their 30s and 40s. To this day the government shells out €10bn a year to the half-million retirees under 50. As you can imagine, the bill for Italian pensioners under 60 years of age is far higher.

Little wonder that Italy has the highest life expectancy in the European Union. The average Italian woman will live – possibly after spending decades claiming benefits – until the age of 85.

Alas, Italy has a debt to GDP rate of 128%. That means the country can barely live within its means, let alone repay its loans, for generations. It's a situation that's spiralling out of control. In Rome late night Metro services are being good. In Verona school English lessons have become a paid-for extra. Something has to give.

But what if *you* wanted to retire like an Italian of old?

To kick back in your forties to a life of Barolo, Prosecco and *spaghetti alle vongole*. To have time to sip a morning cappuccino, take an afternoon siesta and still have time to make love to your husband or wife. Is it a pipe dream?

Italy's top selling novel of all time, *The Leopard*, was set during the Sicilian revolution. In the story, political and economic upheaval smashes class structures in a manner similar to today.

The book's most famous line sums up the predicament that Italy – and the global economy – currently face. "If we want things to stay as they are, things will have to change."

2) Raiders Of The Lost Park

Like it or not we live in a globalised – and increasingly bizarre – financial system. 'Gig economy' staff can create your company logo and deliver your sushi. Virtual currencies like Bitcoin can be used to purchase an app, an airline ticket or a pint of beer. Netflix can provide your daily 'TV' fix even if you don't own a television set. You will almost certainly never meet your bank manager, and may never set eyes on your employer.

Your next car may be driverless. Your next lover may be a machine.

But whatever happens to the global economy, if you own a car parking space in Melbourne, Australia, you may be in luck.

Driveway marketplace Parkhound was formed when Michael Nuciforo and Robert Crocitti were searching for a parking space before an Australian Football League game. They pair thought: "Wouldn't it be great if we could just knock on someone's door and ask to park at their place for a small fee?" The idea stuck.

Australia is big country. Its major cities are ringed by generously proportioned suburbs. Empty driveways abound. "We don't need more parking spaces," explained the duo. "We just need to utilise the parking spaces we already have."

Parkhound is now Australia's Number 1 Car Parking marketplace. Local residents and businesses can upload their parking spaces then lease them out for a few dollars when not in use. Car owners benefit from not having to drive around in circles when an app will point out an empty driveway around the corner.

This AppStore review was written by Lou1546786, a Parkhound driveway owner.

"Thank-god for Parkhound! I'm making money I never thought possible from my empty driveway! Now I can go on a holiday and not stress about my financial situation."

Now what if you had something worth more than a driveway? A garage perhaps. Or a barn. A summerhouse, a spare room, a treehouse or a second home. Or even a space – an office, the spare room of your rented apartment or even your entire home – that wasn't in use for the full 52 weeks a year.

And what if that space could provide an income stream that might not only keep the wolf from the door, but get the wolf so smashed on Barolo and Prosecco that it would never darken your path again?

3) Life in the new economy

The news from Washington and Moscow may be bad. The price of your children's education might keep you awake at night.

But one area of the global economy is growing at such speed that it's paying off mortgages and funding college fees without pausing for breath. We're talking about an economic sector that only became plausible a decade ago, that has furnished pension plans and made a good many people millionaires.

Welcome to the sharing economy, where assets from driveways to empty car commuter seats can be leased to the highest bidder.

The most lucrative part of the sharing economy is short term accommodation rental. Guests who once stayed in bland hotels are looking to let your holiday home, spare room, loft conversion, houseboat, attic space or caravan.

Airbnb saw this opportunity and grabbed it. Like other peer-to-peer property rental websites, hosts upload their Moroccan riad or Singapore studio to the website. Minutes later that property becomes bookable by tens of millions of eager guests across the world. Airbnb handles the transaction and takes a small fee for its service.

The market growth is exponential. As in, on a scale not witnessed in the history of human commerce. In 2010 47,000 guests stayed with Airbnb hosts. In 2015 17 million guests stayed with Airbnb hosts – a growth of 353 times. That single summer this one website handed out $3bn to hosts in Europe alone. That's the same sum as the budget of the Belgian Armed Forces for the entire year.

Just think how much this same portal will hand out to guests *worldwide* in *all* of 2017.

Tonight Airbnb will handle 500,000 stays at 2.3 million listings. These rooms, homes and sleeping spaces are sited in 53,000 towns and cities across the world. You live in, or near, to one of them.

If you're not taking part in this global revolution you are, quite literally, missing out on a large pot of money.

The money is there for the taking. It costs nothing to upload your space.

Join in.

4) Flipping burdens into profit

The two authors of this book come from diverse backgrounds. One is the female CEO of Pebbles, one of France's largest full management holiday rental companies. The first in her family to go to University, after close to a decade of lawyering she gave it up to join forces with her husband and start the business from scratch. The other writer is an award-winning male journalist who has slept in hotels and rental properties hotels in 60 countries.

Between them they have canvassed the thoughts of property owners, city councils and letting agencies on one hand, and magazine editors, economists and politicians on the other.

After several years of research, one story best illustrates a point they hope to make in this book.

In early 2015 Teresa Suarez, a housewife from Albuquerque in New Mexico, packed up the junk from an unused side building attached to her home. She then took the boxes to a self storage depot off the I-40 Interstate highway. The cost of a 20ft (7m) unit was $150 per month. She admits her stuff was all trash: two old TVs, her late mother's library, a dinner set she received as a wedding present in 1998. Sometimes parting with personal effects takes too much effort.

While Suarez was at the storage unit she met two retirees who were clearing out the two boxes they had rented since 1984. That's the year of *Ghostbusters*, *Gremlins* and *Beverly Hills Cop*.

Inside was *real* junk. It was so worthless that the retired couple had forgotten what was inside their two units. Every item they pulled out was a surprise. A bed frame. An electric organ. A Speak & Spell. Roller boots. A collection of dictionaries. A Fisher-Price children's cassette player. A computer monitor where the plastic surround was bigger than the screen.

The price of this luxury? $54,000 per unit over 30 years. Or $108,000 for the pair. The price of fifty luxury cruises or over a hundred return flights to Europe. Up in smoke.

The best bit of the story is what Suarez did next. In late 2015 she renovated her side building to rental standard. Photos were taken and uploaded to three short term rental websites that we'll detail later in this book. She now makes an extra $75 per night from renting out the space, or €450 per week with the discount she offers. That's over $20,000 a year from her previously untapped asset, which had been just sitting there filled with junk for years on end.

In 2017 Suarez is taking a world cruise. She has also thrown away all the junk in her storage unit lest it one day feature in a museum of early 21st-century ephemera.

Her only regret is that she didn't do it sooner.

5) Polish universities, Turkish opthalmologists

Two final missives from the strange economy we inhabit today.

Story one. An English-language college education has become a globalised commodity. Like a Ford Focus or a bag of M&Ms it has an intrinsic value and inherent demand.

After China and India, the world's third biggest outsource country is Poland. Renault car factories and KPMG accountancy desks have relocated to Polish cities like Gdansk and Wroclaw. Here labour is less expensive and English is commonplace.

This year university graduates in England will face average college debts of £44,000 (well over €50,000 or $55,000). That's too shocking for many Brits to contemplate. Chinese and Indians are in the same boat. For students from developing countries planning an English-language education, that's simply too much cash.

That's why all these nationalities have followed Renault and KPMG to Poland. That's right, 50,000 overseas students have 'outsourced' their university years to a land that promises top English-language college courses for minimal cost. With lots of vodka and potatoes thrown in.

In Krakow, Poland's second city, beer is €1 a pint and student dorms cost €80 per month. In Manchester, Britain's second city, beer is £3 a pint (around €3.50) while average student accommodation costs £500 per month (well over €600). European Union students at the Krakow's prestigious University of Economics pay just €1,150 in yearly tuition fees for a Masters Degree in International Business.

The moral of the story is that to maintain standards of living once taken for granted, like a university education for your children, you have to think outside the box.

Google, IBM, Oracle, Motorola, Nokia Siemens, Cisco, Samsung and Uber all maintain offices in Krakow where costs are far lower than back home. These businesses are also thinking outside the box. It might be time for your child to follow them.

Story two. In Scandinavia corrective eye surgery costs around €4,000. In the Turkish coastal city of Izmir doctors use the exact same LASIK laser machines to perform the exact same eye surgery for €1,000 with aftercare included. A burgeoning industry has set up to ferry bespectacled Norwegians from Izmir airport to hospital to their local rental apartment.

Even for issues as essential as healthcare, rich and poor alike must now act differently to make ends meet.

6) Why you need to do it now

The next chapter of this book is actually about short term rental properties.

No Great Depressions. No housewives from New Mexico. No Turkish eye doctors. Promise.

We will use the experience from dozens of rental agencies and hundreds of rental properties to tell you what to offer, what to avoid and how to market yourself.

But you need to do this now. Mansion or spare room. Rich or poor. The longer you stall the more money you lose out on. You have already missed out on the 80 million guests that have booked thus far on Airbnb alone.

Please make your latent space work for you. Make that Mongolian yurt, inherited apartment or Airstream caravan pour money into your bank account day and night. Make it pay over a 10-year period. Or a 30-year one, so that retirement package, or world cruise, or gift to your children is building in your bank account at the rate of tens, if not hundreds, of thousands.

The same lessons apply if you can only rent the property you live in for three weeks this summer while you holiday with friends. Or if you already lease out your second home and want advice distilled from scores of experts on how to make far, far more from that asset. Anyone can join the short term rental revolution.

Times are tough but there are ways and means. People didn't have to rent their driveways in the booming 1960s. But they rarely lived to be 100 years old either.

Increasingly you have to make your own luck. Devise your own future.

In this changing world we have to be clever. To fund the yearly holiday, the television set or the new car we have to think outside the box. Nobody wants to be part of the new poor. A government isn't going to swoop down and give you a helping lift.

But this new era also means anything is possible. If your rental space makes money you might even afford a better car or a better holiday than your boss. That would really be a treat.

The authors of this book joined the short term rental economy many years ago. They have been on this journey countless times and have helped hundreds of others on their way.

It makes no difference to them whether you follow the clear, concise advice laid out in this short book.

It's down to you now.

Do you carry on as normal? Or do you make the change?

Chapter 2 written in stone

1) "If we want things to stay as they are, things will have to change." Sadly, Italy has not changed. Italians cannot afford the same things they could a decade ago.

2) Driveways rent for a few dollars a day. Your home might rent for hundreds of dollars a day.

3) Tonight 500,000 groups will check into rental spaces offered by just one website. If you uploaded your space, some of these eager guests will pay you.

4) Two storage units in Albuquerque cost over $108,000 over 30 years. That's a lot of money to store two vintage TVs and a Garfield bear. It's time to clear a space to make money instead.

5) To maintain living standards you will have to think outside the box. If that means copying Google, IBM, Samsung and Uber, so be it.

6) The tools in this book will help you realise the untapped thousands locked inside your house, garage, garden or second home. If you want to channel that money into your bank account, read on.

Chapter 3: The market blossoms on a thousand branches

"Short term rental agency onefinestay was launched in May 2010 with six London homes. In 2016 it was purchased by AccorHotels for $240m."

> "Growth is never by mere chance; it is the result of forces working together."
>
> **James Cash Penney**

We'll meet the likes of HomeAway, Airbnb and Booking.com in Chapter 4. Mention those three websites and cheap sleeps may spring to mind. But that would be wrong.

Don't think that the short term rental boom is only for random people letting a spare bedroom. Or families offering their home to strangers while they jet off in summer. Oh no.

The market is mushrooming so fast in all directions that, on Airbnb alone, you can book a €9,000 per night chateau in France's Loire Valley as easily as a $9 per night studio in Calcutta, India.

In 2016, pop star Beyoncé stayed in a rented San Francisco villa "with 270 degree views across the bay to all of Silicon Valley". It cost $10,000 per night. She even Instagrammed it. Let's be clear, this rising property rental tide has lifted all ships. Rich or poor, mansion or space room, you can all cash in.

On top of the short lease pile is onefinestay. Like Airbnb user Julie Grover and the Parkhound guys in Australia that we met in Chapter 1, the high-end company all started with a simple idea.

Back in 2009 onefinestay's founder, Greg Marsh, vacationed in Pisa, Italy. He received tips from a local host that made his holiday experience sparkle. On his return he had a second realisation: his luxurious London flat has been empty while he was abroad. Every time he travelled perhaps someone could rent his vacant place. The rest, as they say, is make-somebody-pay-for-your-next-holiday history.

The following paragraph shows – irrefutably – how large the market for non-hotel accommodation has become across all sectors.

onefinestay was launched in May 2010 with six luxurious London homes. During 2011 the business grew tenfold. By 2013 the company was marketing homes in Paris, Los Angeles and New York. In 2016 it was purchased by AccorHotels for $240m with the promise its hospitality business would expand to 40 global cities.

The firm's new CEO Evan Frank sums up his company's niche in this burgeoning market. "We have everything from hip apartments to entire townhouses in our collection. Our homes don't have to be the grandest but they are chosen for space, character and comfort and are always in safe, desirable neighbourhoods. We ultimately ask ourselves 'Would guests love to stay here?'"

The answer is 'yes please'. Unlike Airbnb where almost any space can be uploaded to rent, Frank's team turn down 9 out of 10 prospective properties. Those classy homes that make it onto onefinestay's UK books are furnished with White Company toiletries.

On arrival each guest receives an iPhone pre-installed with local neighbourhood tips. Unlimited calls and data are thrown in. Their portfolio even includes houseboats. You can book its properties directly or through a travel agent, like American Express.

Of course, onefinestay is a niche operator. In this massive new market there is a corner for everyone, be it a garden shed, a yacht or a French chateau. These include Interhome (for holiday accommodation) and Only-Apartments (that markets, erm, apartments only). The vacation website CanadaStays really does do what it says on the tin.

According to Frank: "onefinestay particularly appeals to cases like families, people coming to a city for longer stays and larger groups." Especially those with lots of money.

One piece of Frank's advice is apparent for every host entering this market, prince or pauper alike: "Our rental guests expect personal service every step of the way." It's a lesson to take forward as you ready your property to rent.

Chapter 4: Making your property short rental ready

"Dress to impress, because better property descriptions and photos equal a more lucrative rental asset."

> "A goal without a plan is just a wish."
>
> **Antoine de Saint-Exupéry**

The plans are in place. By using the calculator and some rental apps on your iPhone you've fantasised about your second income, early retirement or world cruise. You have a vague but promising idea of how much extra income could net.

You're close. In fact, there's just one step to go before you click the button to start advertising your spare room, Balinese villa or Budapest apartment around the world.

Sadly, that's as exciting as this chapter gets. If you were expecting *Girl On The Train*, *The Alchemist* or *Live And Let Die* we're sorry to disappoint. But the information corralled into this chapter is the distilled knowledge gleaned from hundreds of rental properties across the globe.

Essentially, this chapter will point out what tasks to do now to turn your property into rental gold. We're confident it will save you a fortune in time and money later on.

1) Walk a thousand miles in your guests' shoes

The key factor when planning what to put inside your rental space is to put yourself in the shoes of a paying rental guest. Wear their Uggs, Doc Martins or Nikes for an entire day. If you would personally splash out on a rental apartment with a great looking kitchen and bathroom – or refuse to rent a place without Wi-Fi or comfy sofas – then you have great insight into your prospective client base.

So ask yourself, what sort of guests are going to stay and what sort of furniture/equipment/fittings are going to appeal?

Put simply, the better equipped your property – be it a mountain hut in Chile or a cosy flat in Edinburgh – the better its description and photos will be. And better descriptions and photos equal a more lucrative rental asset for you.

Be painfully aware that there may be thousands of properties in your area. Therefore, most guests narrow down their search by clicking checkboxes or filters on their rental booking website.

Often these will depend on where your rental space is located. In the area of Nice, France, the two highest sought out amenities are air-conditioning and outside space, closely followed by a sea view. This stands to reason when a guest is spending time in a sunny seaside city. On dedicated ski resort websites filters include log fires, hot tubs and saunas.

You get the picture. In a crowded rental space like Sydney or Vienna, properties that tick as many filter boxes as possible are the ones with a far better chance of securing the most bookings.

Of course, you can't magic up outside space and a sauna. But you can tick amenities like Wi-Fi, washing machine, dishwasher and baby cots. All four of those items are regularly 'check-boxed' by searching travellers, particularly by families and large groups.

The most important check-box there is? Wi-Fi. It's universally expected. A high-speed connection not only allows guests to stay in touch on email, Skype and WhatsApp, but also to watch the latest Jeremy Clarkson shenanigans on Amazon. Not to mention cartoons for their children on YouTube and The Crown on Netflix. All guests carry a smartphone; the majority now travel with a Kindle, iPad or laptop too.

If you could install Wi-Fi for $30 a month but opt not to, then simply put, you are a fool. It's the filter than everybody and their mother ticks, and your property won't show up on most detailed searches without it.

At the Pebbles rental agency in Nice, many self-employed guests book stays in our least popular months for four to eight weeks at a time. They want to work at 'home', see a bit of the world and write off their cost as a business expense. Quite a few writers have perfected their books, and many financial traders have played the stock markets from our apartments. They wouldn't have entertained staying without Wi-Fi. Nor would parents with an iPhone addiction – for either themselves or their kids.

2) Styling your main living space for rental success

Essential for nearly every rental property is a flat screen TV and Wi-Fi. You are welcome to offer more advanced entertainment facilities from iPads to Bluetooth stereos. But fail to provide these basics, or supply defective models, and your guests (who have paid a premium for hotel standard accommodation) will call you or email you to ask either where they are or why they don't work. It's not a nice conversation to have.

Remember that many of your potential guests scan photos of scores of apartments and they make quick judgement calls. If your living area boasts a 1990s big box TV (remember those?) they might immediately ignore your place thinking that the rest of the space hasn't been touched since Bill Clinton was president (remember those days too?). Why risk that happening when an outlay of some $400 will get you a new model? Chances are your guests won't turn on the TV the whole time they stay, but that's not the point we're making.

Brits buy houses based on garden space all the time. They dream of summer BBQs, their kids playing with the hosepipe around the lawn. Chances are the weather gods will inundate the British Isles with another inglorious summer of soggy chips and Wimbledon downpours. But they will still predicate a house purchase by the size of the exterior space: and they'll still look for grand garden when they book a property to rent.

If your rental space can fit a sofa (you can leave your Mongolian yurt or converted train carriage out of this equation) then buy a top quality one that has a practical covering that will look good when photographed. This will be worth the extra expense. Don't cover it with a fabric throw on the photos. That just screams at a guest you are trying to cover something up. Sofas suffer natural wear and tear so you need to budget for professional cleaning on a regular basis. Decorative cushions should have removable covers that can be regularly washed.

For anything other than a budget market try to avoid fold-out beds like futons. Even if they are not hard and lumpy, they look it – and remind guests of their blissed-out student days. Late arrivals don't want to assemble their bed at 10pm, then dissemble it each morning. They'd rather be exploring a museum, market or beach. Hotels have not abandoned the traditional bed in favour of sofa-beds for good reason.

Complaints arise when property owners don't provide comfortable seating for as many people as the apartment can sleep. If your apartment accommodates four, then you need sofas to comfortably seat four plus a dining table for four. If not, your guests will complain and could request a partial refund. There are no excuses.

What's more, most moms (and this demographic books

more holidays and weekends away than the rest) will count seating before booking. If your photos don't prove that four guests can sit in the living area without a child on someone else's knee, she's going to jettison your space and move on.

Without a coffee table your living area photo will lack a good frame. Even if you decide the room really doesn't warrant one, prepare for more damage and wear and tear than you might otherwise have prevented. Guests will either balance mugs on sofa armrests, or leave glasses on the floor. Don't risk it. Choose a design which is stylish yet robust as it's something that will be used a lot by those staying in your apartment. The duo behind this book have managed the cleaning up after 15,000 short-term stays. We know what we're talking about.

Never underestimate the benefits of plenty of soft furnishings and decorative pieces such as artwork, mirrors, cushions and rugs. These make your rental property or spare room a home.

However, you don't have to spend a fortune on these finishing touches to make the apartment look alluring on the photos you will upload to a property booking website like HomeAway, HolidayLettings or Airbnb, which we'll detail in the following chapter. Moreover, we strongly recommend that you don't fill the apartment with expensive antique pieces, designer artworks or limited edition prints. Yep, just leave the Rothko canvas and the Dali sculpture in the safe.

3) Let there be light

This often-overlooked item is critically important. Fortunately, it's not expensive to get right. Take a look round your space and think what all guests, not just you, would want. You might not read in the living area, but a guest might. Therefore, they need a reading lamp. At dusk they might want a light that exudes ambiance and romance, not a fluorescent tube in the kitchen. Dimmer switches work well and are often inexpensive to install.

Check that the main lights are sufficient in the evening, especially in the kitchen over food preparation areas. Purchase some standing lamps if necessary. Guests commonly damage lamps as they may be knocked over by accident. Choose a stylish design but don't go Bill Gates. At some point they may well need to be replaced.

For bedroom lighting, consider what you want out of a hotel room, then expect to provide the same for your guests. Who wants to drown in bright light when reading in bed? Dim bedside lamps are a must.

If the bedroom sleeps two, try to not send your guests to the nearest Relate counsellor when they get home. Not everyone has moved onto Kindle backlit reading. Many still like good Penguin books in bed (with the light on) while their other half sleeps, which necessitates two lamps, not one.

Not everyone enjoys sex in the pitch black. Nor do they want the overhead lamps to blaze like a shopping mall. Make sure you offer somewhere in between.

If lights cannot be dimmed in a bedroom, your guests are going to have to improvise. We have seen them do this a thousand times by moving the light on the floor and putting a cover, book or pillow on top of the fitting. What a shame to risk damage to your furnishings or even a fire, when all you need is a few low wattage bulbs.

4) Everything and the kitchen sink

Kitchens are the most time-consuming room to furnish. Pebbles give their hosts a checklist of items guests expect to find in an average food preparation and eating area. Naturally, while what is required depends on the size of the property, the kitchen space and the number of guests for whom you are providing, there are some absolute essentials.

As a guide, large appliances usually include a refrigerator, oven, extractor fan, washing machine, dryer, dishwasher and vacuum cleaner. Smaller items usually include wine glasses, tumblers, corkscrew, bottle opener, tin opener, kitchen knives, cutlery, utensils, scissors, pans, baking tray, roasting tin, frying pan, saucepans, salt and pepper set, dinner plates, side plates, bowls, egg cups, mugs, kettle, simple cafetière or French press coffee maker, chopping board, colander, tea towels, toaster, teapot, serving jug, cheese grater, microwave, scales, sieve, storage containers, measuring jug, potato peeler, rubbish bin and clothes drying rack. Plus, an iron, ironing board, mop and bucket, doormat, dustpan and brush.

Got that? You don't have to spend the earth but if an average rental property doesn't contain 95% of the above then negative reviews (see Chapter 10) can and will commence. Even if a guest does not bother you to provide the missing essentials right now, and might not even complain, they will remember. If your space has any competition, they might just try that other place the second time around.

Guests also need a supply of bulbs for the various lights throughout the apartment. You have to purchase these anyway so buy half a dozen of each. If these aren't supplied guests will complain – and you will still have to buy them, visit the property to install them *and* deal with a negative review.

At Pebbles we photograph every lamp in each property, then offer a printed guide to how to change the light bulb. It's so simple, but has saved both us and our property owners thousands of trips to the apartment or the store. Light bulbs are a great example that planning ahead and setting up a system in advance will pay off later on.

5) A sob story

To focus the point we just made, we're going to labour it. As in really labour the hell out of it with a sob story.

So, picture the scene. Imagine a guest is at your apartment, villa or penthouse ready to cook. He or she has purchased fresh scallops, a bottle of Chardonnay and a can of tuna for dinner. Then they discover at the dinner hour that there is unfortunately no chopping knife/corkscrew/can opener. Miss just one of these items and you're going to get the call, or your agent is.

You're going to have to drop what you are doing, don your red cape and go and source and deliver the item so your guests can enjoy their dinner (even if your evening meal is now in the dog). Your also now at risk of compensating them for the groceries they bought and the cost of eating dinner out.

It doesn't matter that there was a can-opener there last month when you visited. Nor does it matter if the corkscrew is there now but the guest can't find it. Whoever deals with your property, has to deal with that missing item to satiate that guest.

Did we mention the guest is a Michelin starred chef? Or that he was about to propose a declaration of marriage over dinner? Ok, we laboured too far, but we're making this point because not only is this an easy way to keep most guests happy, you will save so much money, time and hassle. Sourcing at short notice ALWAYS costs far more than having double supplies.

By their very nature short term holiday lets incur costs for replacing everyday items, either due to wear and tear or loss. Knives become blunt. Pans become burnt and scratched. Teaspoons go missing. Whether they have or they haven't, guests believe they have paid a lot for their stay and they want the problem fixed right away.

It can pay to be well stocked – even overstocked – on these top 12 items, which our experience proves are the most regularly reported as needing to be replaced:

1. Frying Pans 2. Teaspoons 3. Chopping boards 4. Small sharp knifes 5. Saucepans 6. Deep cereal bowls 7. Oven roasting dishes 8. Corkscrews 9. Can openers 10. Oven gloves 11. Scissors 12. Large bread knife.

When guests leave, send them an email asking for their advice. Did they feel any of the items in your property needed replacing or were missing? They're often more than happy to tell you, and it proves you care. You'll then know in advance what to stock. It's called a win-win.

6) Bedrooms and bathrooms

Bedrooms are about beds and a good night's sleep. You provide both by the best quality and biggest bed that the space allows. Plus good lighting (as mentioned in point three).

Let's start with an example. British motel Travelodge appeals to budget travellers or business travellers. But it's made a huge marketing success of claiming that all their rooms have a comfy king size bed designed exclusively for them by Sleepeezee with 950 individual pocket springs and four plump pillows. They've even trademarked it 'the Travelodge Dreamer'.

Their marketing is spot on. No one cares about soft furnishings or toiletries if the bed doesn't assure a solid night's sleep. Nothing makes us sigh for lost opportunity like when we see a property rental photo of a standard double bed in a large bedroom. Think of how your prospective guests may view with same dull image. It's hardly a hotel is it?

As we'll see in chapter 6, guests tend to book short term rental properties as they would a hotel – and treat them like one. Essential items for bedrooms include two pillows for each person (ideally one soft, one hard), waterproof mattress and pillow protectors, duvet, bedside tables with drawers, bedroom reading lights, coat hangers, wardrobe/storage space for hanging clothes and a full length mirror.

Optional bedroom items include cushions to decorate the beds, small rug if the floor is tiled, throws to dress the beds, pictures on the walls and hooks on back of doors. Make sure guests have enough space to hang their clothes on clothes hangers. Again, put yourself in your guests' shoes. Sleep a night in your rental space. Unpack in there. Undress in there. Read in the bed. The object is to offer everything a guest will need to keep them writing great reviews, telling their friends and booking again.

Finally, check how dark the room is at night. Are the shutters/curtains/blinds sufficient or does the light come through? Guests on holiday, business trips or party weekends don't want to wake up at sunrise.

Bathroom essentials include a mirror, toothbrush holder, toilet roll holder, a shelf to put toiletries on near the basin, plus a shelf to put shampoo on inside the shower cubicle. There's nothing worse than having a shower and having to put your shower gel on the floor. It's not student-land.

Guests also need a soap dish, waste bin, towel rail, high-powered hairdryer, hooks, a lock on the door, bath mats and mirror. If you have a glass shower screen, then check the seal on it. Floors can be very slippery if the seal is not perfect as the shower water may leak onto the floor causing all sorts of mayhem.

7) How boring is this chapter going to get?

Want to read the bit where we start talking about hard cash? Well, you'd better read this bit first. Keeping a rental space clean garners great reviews but is the planet's dullest time-suck. Here's how to keep this key task efficient.

Finally, if any family members harbour doubts about your cleanliness, call a professional cleaner. If you must go it alone, here are five top tips gleaned from years of scrubbing up to 15 apartments per day.

1) Cleaning up after short term guests 'should' be easy. You ought to be cleaning an uncluttered space, free of personal belongings. Make sure your rental area isn't jam-packed with crap, pap and dusty *objets d'art* before you start.

2) With a set sequence in mind you can surface clean a 30m2 (320sqft) space in an hour. We'd advise setting a stopwatch for 60 minutes, plus another 30 in which to

tackle a job you have neglected for a while. Like wiping down cupboards, dusting doorframes, cleaning out the heating vent. You can't neglect these little things for too long.

3) Take care of bigger jobs on a rota. For example, unless there's been a sandstorm, tsunami or Act of God you shouldn't have to clean the outside windows every single week. Cleaning skirting boards, on top of picture frames and inside the cutlery drawer might only need doing every month.

4) There are lots of time saving cleaning devices on the market. Our favourite is a Wi-Fi enabled robot vacuum cleaner. A host may have a surprise last-minute booking while on business in Lusaka, Zambia, then turn on their vacuum cleaner in Suva, Fiji several thousand miles away. The vacuum maps out a specific floor area and cleans way better than a human can. At around $500 it's an investment that's seriously worth it when you consider 50 cleans per year. That works out at $10 a time for a job you don't have to do.

5) Steam mops and steam cleaners make light work and can keep your place looking newer for longer. They also make grout and floor tiles shine like the Tom Cruise's teeth. Tom Cruise is good. Remember Cocktail? Remember Top Gun??? Good.

8) The keys to success

On a Sunday (it's always on a Sunday, trust us) hapless guests leave their set of keys hanging from the lock on the back of the door. They then rush out to enjoy one last hazy and happy breakfast before rushing back to pack and catch their 10-hour long haul flight. Breakfast service is slow but no matter. They are in good spirits and good time. They'll throw their clothes into their suitcases along with all their cares in the world. Oh how nice this city is, how we don't want to leave, we must book that cute little property again.

They stroll back, and discover they should be careful what they wish for. They can't get back in. They call you (you may live in the same city; you may live in a different time zone). You explain while you or your agent will try and get the matter sorted, it's Sunday and you need a heavy-duty locksmith to get that solid metal door open. You try but fail to get a locksmith before their plane leaves the runway. Six people miss their flights at €800 euros a time, and they miss their daughter's graduation for good measure.

Faced with this scenario the guests might accept it was their fault. But equally they might not. They might dispute the amount paid with their credit card provider. Or threaten legal action because they claim that the key "broke in the door" or "got jammed in the broken lock". Unless you can prove them wrong (which is where good instructions come in) you're left with a door to fix at the very least. Worse still, another far heftier payment could rest with you too.

Be it a spare room, an entire apartment or the entrance to your building, you need to get your locks right. Most property rental agents require five (yes, five!) sets of keys. That's three for guests, plus two for the manager/cleaner/agent/plumber/emergency key-holder to deal with issues as they arise. If you have one of those fancy locks with keys that cost $100 a time to cut, now might be time to change the locks.

People have a lot of success with keypad combination locks, which can be changed by the guest. These are excellent choices if renting a spare room. You can override the keypad in an emergency, but only that guest can get inside. You can keep security high by changing the code often; conversely you can't change keys often without incurring a lot of expense. If your space can fit a combination lock, we highly recommend it.

In our experience the best solution is to purchase a door lock that shuts behind guests when they depart. They can leave their set of keys (one of five, yes five sets you have in reserve) on the kitchen table instead of in the letterbox, which is asking for trouble.

On a final note make sure locks work fluidly. Give them an oil often. Locks seem to have a habit of finally giving up on Sundays when it costs double to call a locksmith. If guests can't get back in, you may have a hefty hotel bill to pay, as well as compensation plus the locksmith charge. We've known owners to suffer a €1,000 bill when the lock broke on a Sunday evening. Don't let it be you.

Chapter 4 written in stone

1) Would you refuse to rent a place without Wi-Fi or a serviceable kitchen? Put yourself in your customer's shoes to gain insight into your prospective client base.

2) Planning, planning, planning. Getting your rental space ready necessitates a lot of lists. But certain standards must be reached before the money starts rolling in.

3) Lighting, lighting, lighting. Nobody wants to have sex in a shopping mall.

4) Buying all the items that your kitchen space requires will drive you mad. But if you fail to make an IKEA order, stock up with dinner sets from a family member, or even purchase your equipment second-hand, your guest will also go mad. And you will have to deal with it.

5) See point four. Unless you want us to labour it again for you...

6) Offering a good night's sleep is key to a full calendar, good reviews and repeat custom. Sleep there yourself to see if there's anything that could be improved.

7) To earn hard cash you need to clean hard. There are ways and means of expediting the task.

8) Unless you own a castle (in which case guests will need even more keys) you should have five sets within your grasp. Make sure the locks work. And double check that guests know how the locks work. If your keys fail spectacularly on a Sunday evening, it will be your problem, not your guests'.

Chapter 5: A carefully staged photo shoot speaks a thousand words

"PhotoShop can only go so far."

> "You don't take a photograph, you make it."
>
> **Ansel Adams**

"It's not about selling a property," says award-winning photographer Rebecca Marshall. "It's about using your images to sell a lifestyle."

Marshall should know. She has photographed some of the world's finest homes for clients like the New York Times, the FT and Der Spiegel. These include artist Jean Cocteau's former villa in the South of France, and the penthouse suite atop Monaco's La Tour Odeon, at $355m the most expensive apartment in the world.

It takes Marshall between 30 minutes and an hour to 'stage' each room before she even removes her lens cap. She advises you to do the same when photographing your rental space, be it a spare room or Bavarian castle. "I've had clients bring in fresh croissants, bottles of chilled rosé and copies of hip magazines to set the scene inside their apartment. These additions won't be the focus of your shot, but will add flavour and tangibility to the image you are trying to convey."

Offering such an image is key. Because when potential guests scroll through hundreds of available properties, they scan the main photo and read the headline, before shortlisting a list of 'possibles' for their summer vacation, city break or business trip.

Professional photographers like Marshall will utilise anything that lends a sense of place. A background view from a window in the living room. A photo of the local beach in a picture frame on a desk. An antique mirror that offers a sense of timeless class, while reflecting the other side of the room being photographed.

On bigger shoots Marshall corrals a team of assistants to porter lighting and flash bulbs. In smaller places she simply switches on every single light, and opens every window as far as possible, to bring the image to life. "You should even turn on the light on the extractor fan above the oven."

She then walks around the room slowly planning what shot will take in what items. Perhaps the bed plus its side table with reading glasses and vintage guidebook on them. Or the kitchen table with breakfast laid out next to a copy of *The Times*, *Hello!*, *Vanity Fair*, or whatever journal your clientele is likely to read.

Then the shooting starts. Marshall urges every property photographer to use a tripod for a cleaner, sharper, straighter image. "The cost from €25 and you can instantly tell when someone hasn't used one."

She uses a wide-angle lens to give each property a sense of space. "But not a fish-eye as these will distort your room and can make it look cheap."

The better the photos, the more sordid details are shown up. If bed sheets are askew or if carpets are slightly stained the camera doesn't lie. "PhotoShop can only go so far," says Marshall. "So making your place perfect before the shoot is 75% of the job in hand." If the property you are uploading to HolidayLettings has four bedrooms, you're in for a long day.

Marshall has one final tip. "The key main image that forms the pointed end of your marketing strategy must represent your rental property's USP." If it has a great pool, place it in the foreground with property behind it. If you have a small funky studio, keep it clear but with every addition laid out like the folding bed, BOSE stereo, iPad, art book library and espresso machine. "This takes time," says Marshall, "but there's no way around it."

The customer on the other side of the world, with their credit card in hand, wants to see it all. Now comes the exciting bit.

Chapter 6: Make your rental listing work doubly hard

"Getting the right advertising mix for your rental property would drive the marketing director of Coca-Cola insane."

"You can't sell anything if you can't tell anything".

Beth Comstock

Choices, choices, choices. How do you tell the world about your glamorous new tent complex, container home or villa? Your property photos look fabulous but where should you upload them to?

When you decide to rent your property it seems the path to extra income leads to Airbnb via TripAdvisor plus an advert in your local supermarket.

But then your friend at work tells you about Owners Direct, or that VRBO has an introductory offer that includes extra photos and a translation of your rental page into German, Spanish and Portuguese.

And another friend, who has been renting his place in Cancun on Mexico's Riviera Maya since the 1990s, swears by using a local agency. The agent cleans up after your guests. And they also take their own photos and manage all advertising as part of their fee.

Getting the right advertising mix for your rental property would drive the marketing director of Coca-Cola insane.

In the first instance keep one word in mind. Mud.

1) The market becomes muddy

Back in 2005 the short term letting industry was in in its infancy. There were big booking sites like HomeAway and Villarentals but they only had about 50 to 100 properties in each destination. Now they each have thousands upon thousands in most cities across the world.

By 2010 the waters were muddier than Glastonbury Festival after a British downpour. The worldwide sites that had previously stuck to hotels – including TripAdvisor, Booking.com and Lastminute.com – were advertising short term rental properties.

Over the past few years, other websites including Airbnb, Wimdu and Housetrip – plus hundreds of others that we're not going to waste time listing here – have come from nowhere to become, in some cases, massive players.

It's clear to all is that the holiday rental sector is booming. It's a huge industry worldwide. But the difference between 2005 and 2017 is that millions, rather than hundreds, of people are buying/converting/decorating some sort of second home/caravan/shed. And it's not only holiday apartments but city apartments, houseboats and even treehouses in the Amazon jungle.

For example, many new hosts are hard-up homeowners who want to rent out their spare room. Hotels are also having to compete and are coming to the market with apart-hotels that they advertise on Airbnb and the like.

It's all very confusing.

Fortunately for you, over the last decade we've checked out the planet's top 20 short term letting websites. We've also testing the 'big four' property portals to breaking point and interviewed dozens of clients who rely on them.

2) Why we both love and hate Airbnb

There's no denying some people love Airbnb. The most well known of the 'big four' short term letting websites has become a household name. One of the authors of this book swears by the company. The other author of this book still thinks it's more advertising hype than substance. The first author rents a lovely, quirky apartment. The second author manages high-end rental properties that command a higher nightly rate.

It's true that some previous hosts have shut the door on Airbnb and changed their locks for good. Airbnbhell.com lists "Uncensored Airbnb Stories & Reasons Not To Use Airbnb" and has been featured in The Guardian, BuzzFeed and Vanity Fair.

Some of the site's comments are from users. Choice postings include: "Terrible Bed, Dildo in Nightstand". Common owners' comments include: "Airbnb Cancellation Policy is Unfair to Hosts". You can probably guess what else is on the website but it's worth a visit if you're renting your property for the first time.

Now, no company becomes as big as Airbnb without upsetting a few characters along the way. Nor is there any such thing as bad publicity, within reason. If they're talking about you, and millions of people are using your website, you're doing something right.

Many people, be they guests or owners, have excessively high expectations about what any web portal can offer. When stripped down from the hype everyone knows they are unlikely to be booking the same pad as celebrity Airbnb endorser Beyoncé. In most cases they are just hoping to get a standard place to stay if they are a guest, or a regular guest staying if they are a host.

Which all serves to say, if you're a realist and accept that all transactions come with a certain amount of calculated risk, then you're good to go. You need to understand that there is only so much a web portal can do, and the rest is going to be up to you.

No website's booking fees are cheap. Neither are Airbrb's. For a €1,500 per week apartment booking Airbnb will charge the guest about €1,675, thus a €175 cut. It will then distribute around €1,445 to the host, thus another €55 cut. Multiply that over hundreds of thousands of bookings per year and it's no wonder the company is valued at $30bn, more than Hilton Hotels.

Our mixed experience with Airbnb is that customers are generally looking for a keenly priced property. Pebbles found they were fielding requests from potential guests wanting to pay between €50 and €200 a night too frequently for it to be worthwhile for the agency. This s changing – leading British Newspapers The Times and The Daily Mail recently ran 'The World's Top 10 Airbnb Properties' stories. Remember the story about Beyoncé's Airbnb pad in chapter 3? Yet the firm has roots in the millennial collaborative economy and it will always struggle to shed its reputation as an easy-to-book portal for funky bargains.

Furthermore, Airbnb's policy seems to be 'no agents'. Certainly Pebbles aren't allowed to list, even if they wanted to. We can't find high class operation onefinestay on there either. With pressure from various governments they are steadfast in marketing themselves as 'people renting out a room on a peer-to-peer basis', rather than commercia landlords or agents.

As much of the best property stock in each city is wrapped up with quasi-hotel style agencies (like onefinestay and Pebbles) when you have a superb offering of a full home, then most often an agency will be better suited to your needs. More on that later.

Airbnb have an advertising budget and a word-of-mouth value like no other. They also have gazillions of listings all competing to be seen. Before listing, look at how full booking calendars are and how much competition there is. The less competition the better otherwise you could get lost in the crowd. If you do find the space crowded, the way to stand out is to price cheap, at least until your positive reviews flow in – as we'll read about in chapter 10.

In short. Airbnb is for you if you want to list anything from a spare bedroom to a Philippine beach shack for free in the next few hours, with a view to taking bookings tomorrow. It might not be for you if you host a high class apartment and don't want to field emails-a-plenty offering to rent your space for below the advertised price.

One final note. Can I advertise my penthouse apartment on Airbnb (or other web portal site) as well as with an agent? The short answer is yes, if the agency doesn't mind. Advertising your rental space on more than one website will obviously increase the amount of people that view your property.

However, make sure you guard against double bookings, which are an embarrassing hellhole to dig yourself out from.

The price of your property posted by Airbnb and its competitors will include a premium, so if a prospective client sees your place advertised for two different figures it may damage trust.

Finally, Airbnb's terms and conditions may also contradict your agency's legal terms and obligations, so be aware of this going forward.

3) What about HolidayLettings, the TripAdvisor company?

If you haven't heard of TripAdvisor, then the Obama Presidency must have also passed you by. The holiday review website is more widely travelled than Air Force One. And the site now offers a fast-growing short term booking apartment service known as HolidayLettings too.

TripAdvisor's HolidayLettings rental portal is big on visitor numbers and properties listed. It has 5,000 in New York alone. However, the sheer number of listings can affect booking ratios. All 180 Pebbles properties are listed on the website, but it can take an hour to find a Pebbles property. Pebbles receive just a handful of enquiries a week from TripAdvisor with a conversion-to-booking ratio of around 5%. Pricing may have something to do with it. Depending on your offering, this might not be a good enough conversion rate if this is the only place you list.

From a service point of view, since 2016 we've found HolidayLettings cumbersome to work with. Hosts cannot talk to a guest on the telephone until HolidayLettings have confirmed the booking (and pocketed the fee that goes with it).

Conversing on email via the website's booking system is the only way to chat. Feedback is that guests have found the booking process of email only as frustrating as the host. Every customer service trainer will stress how the phone is often a great tool for customers, and it's a real shame this is now lost.

When you've been at this a while, you will build up standard email signatures when dealing with same questions time and time again. Great for time management. Sadly, as you can only communicate through the TripAdvisor platform, emails are harder, and so conversations get shorter. Again, the guest loses out. The type of guest who uses this platform tends to have more questions and does more research than the happy-go-lucky Airbnb types. This can lead to less customer satisfaction even before they've got the keys. Misunderstandings can more easily occur and sometimes the guest feels misled about the booking, which an agency or an individual would have been able to correct had they been able to speak to the client directly prior to booking.

The back interface of the HolidayLettings website can crash. It sometimes crashes when in the middle of correspondence with a guest or a photo upload. The response time, the reviews and the prices occasionally go haywire, which can damage your hard-earned reputation. Pebbles spent hundreds of wasted manpower working with TripAdvisor's HolidayLettings portal in 2016 alone; a few hours should have done the job sufficiently.

On the plus side, this web portal is the leader in review gathering. The guests who go through this site read and write reviews. This core clientele is the pickiest of the bunch, and if you have a great offering, and follow the advice in this book, then this site is a great way to secure those all important five star reviews. (It's also the easiest place to pick up one star reviews too – but we'll show you how to handle those in chapter 10).

In short. HolidayLettings is for you if you want to "List your home with the world's largest travel community". It's free to do so and guarantees a large audience. Like Airbnb they charge a commission from a host's payment, 3% in this case. They also charge a mammoth levy on every guest's booking - from 5% to 15% of the total booking value.

One final note. Most short term booking websites like HolidayLettings and Airbnb ask you to choose a cancellation policy. Less conservative settings allow guests to cancel the day before they arrive. Stricter settings might mean that guests are entitled to a 50% refund if they cancel 60 days before check-in.

In our experience very few bookers have a habit of changing their dates or abandoning their reservation. Some 97% of Pebbles guests don't ask to alter their booking after a deposit have been sent. After all, your property is most likely a unique space that can't be booked elsewhere, rather than a standard hotel room that can be re-reserved at the last minute. Quite logically, larger groups tend to cancel less. After all, who would want to rearrange multiple sets of flights, airport transfers and travel calendars?

We recommend that you go with a 'strict' policy on your holiday rental website if you have a superb or rare offering and your price is high. In our experience it won't put people off bookings and will form a guard against any sob stories (and subsequent refunds) the day before your guests are due to check-in.

We'd recommend a less stringent policy if your space is more standard, you have a lot of competition and you can't live with losing a couple of hundred pounds. Your competition is more likely to be hotels, an accommodation option that guests are used to cancelling at the last minute. That you can also offer late cancellation might be the thing that swings it for them booking your space over someone else's.

4) VRBO/HomeAway/OwnersDirect, the all-in-one website that delivers

Like Justin Bieber, VRBO is a global phenomenon. Although still young it feels like it's been around for years. Its name is known across scores of nations. The website's fans – let's call them VRBeliebers – find it time tested and ever-popular.

What this portal has is volume. The site reaches 44 million monthly travellers across the world because it advertises globally. VRBO is marketed internationally as HomeAway. In British newspapers it advertises itself as OwnersDirect. It sponsored the EURO2016 European football championship as Abritel/HomeAway. In Australia the site is known as Stayz. Many Germans will book their next holiday home in Mallorca on FeWo-direkt. Of course, these brands are all the same big beast of a website that feeds in millions of customers and bookings into the VRBO/HomeAway giant. It's effective and simple-to-use – but it does cost a small fortune to advertise on.

Just like the controversial Canadian minstrel, VRBO has changed its appearance over the years. It used to be a simple 'pay up and post your pics' website. Then it started charging in bands for more prominent positions.

Finally, VRBO has evolved into a two-option operation: you can simply pay a hefty fee up front for a listing, or pay a massive fee (minimum 8%) for each booking you take. For this you will get "visibility" on their 25 top international sites. Beware: visibility means it's listed, but finding your property might be like trying to find your goldfish in the Mississippi.

Pebbles listed properties on HomeAway and its subsites between 2007 and 2016. In the good old days, HomeAway was a superb web portal to list with. Then our goldfishes got lost in the lake and the cost of listing outweighed the benefits.

If you think your property will get lost, the answer might be pay-per-booking. You've heard that you should never pay for a trade job upfront right? Once you have, there's less incentive for the worker.

By electing this option, VRBO have to work for their money. We'd guess that this means your listing might get priority on certain algorithms despite the marketing saying that an upfront yearly fixed fee is better. If you add the booking fee onto your price, you have nothing to lose.

In short. VRBO is for you if you have a fairly standard apartment or villa that you want to rent to a fairly traditional audience. The portal has an army of loyal followers who have used them for more than a decade.

One final note. Most booking websites have an 'Instant Book' option. This means that you allow website viewers to reserve your property with their credit cards without going through endless emails back and forth. Each website will promise that 'you will get 60% more bookings if you switch on Instant Booking' or some such statistic. Do you know what? They're right.

Some guests, including both the authors' mothers, will send endless back and forth emails before they make a firm booking. But a significant minority of guests prefer to reserve a nice looking property without any hassle – just as they would book a hotel online. Again, in our experience it's younger (possibly time poor) guests booking smaller properties (perhaps ones that don't require too many advance questions) that tend to use Instant Booking. Older guests booking a multiple-bedroomed property for a family with varying needs tend to liaise back and forth beforehand.

Does Instant Book open you up to all sorts of weirdos? No. Because Instant Book is a misnomer. It doesn't actually mean a guest can instantly book your property. As an owner you will first receive an alert or an email that tells you about the booking – which you have the right to cancel over the coming 24 hours on most websites, Airbnb included. We therefore advise you to turn Instant Booking on.

5) Booking.com, the one that pours hotel guests in to your spare room

Booking.com is 21 years old. In real life it would be old enough to drink whisky, smoke cigarettes and make love with abandon.

The web giant has a million properties, most of them hotels, under contract. That's so many options that customers don't need to browse any other another website when looking for a hotel in Dallas, Texas or Busan, Korea. They really are that big.

Tonight Booking.com will handle near on a million room reservations. That's far more than Airbnb. In part that's because of a new wave of 'white label' partnerships that it offers to airlines like Europe's easyJet. When you book a city centre suite after reserving your flight to London, Booking.com are behind the transaction and easyJet takes a small cut.

Can you guess what's front of mind at the HQ of Booking.com's parent company Priceline in Norwalk, Connecticut? Your health? Your best interests? Don't be silly. Priceline is a global behemoth with operations in 200 countries and $10bn in annual revenue. It's even bigger than Booking.com and it certainly doesn't sweat the small stuff.

What those who advertise their short let properties on Booking.com receive is something very special. We're talking more exposure than a glamour model on an all-day shoot. Since 2015 the all-encompassing web portal began listing homestays like apartments and villas alongside hotel-style accommodation.

Some statistics report that Booking.com has the highest customer satisfaction ratings. This is for guests, not hosts like you. Booking.com is all about pricing. It's all about their commission. Their cut is often 17% or higher depending on your agreement. Yep, 17% for just taking a booking that you are then tied into. The portal even reserves the right to automatically resell a room that one of its customers has cancelled. To protect their commission, the customer's email address is hidden from the host to prevent any direct contact.

Some hosts (mainly hoteliers) are fighting back, but arguably too late. The European Union has warned that Booking.com and fellow internet firms Facebook and Google might reach "a point of no return" where they become the only player in town. There are dozens of sites and posts to read if you type phrases like "boycott booking.com".

Many establishments have now become so dependent on the site that they can't leave without staring bankruptcy in the face. Not that that's Booking.com's fault. They are just exceptionally good at what they do. If you do advertise with them it's worth marketing elsewhere too, just to keep your options open.

Finally, Booking.com protect their reputation for the best pricing at all costs. When you sign up, your contract states that you will not advertise lower prices on your own site or any other marketing channels than are quoted on

Booking.com. There are penalties ranging from fines to expulsion if you do. The other main rental portals are often less restrictive. Firstly, by using Airbnb or VRBO it means that you can price higher or lower on your own website according to your needs. Secondly, the price promise means that if you do intend to work with several different accommodation websites, this might hinder your contractual arrangement with Booking.com.

In short. Booking.com is for you if own or manage hotel style accommodation in a city centre that dovetails with the website's regular user needs. You'll need competitive prices to get a look-in. This might mean selling your soul and forgetting about doing the smaller things that show you care about your pad. If you plan to market a tiny farmhouse in the boondocks where you throw in a hands-on cow milking session, forget it. With a site this size you trade massive exposure for a relative lack of customer control. And as Booking.com's clients are frequently price-led, you may not always get the nicest ones booking your precious place.

One final note: The relative monopoly of Booking.com is a worldwide issue and is outside the scope of this book. Governments are concerned and pressure groups are lobbying. For now Booking.com arguably enjoy virtually unchallenged market conditions where they can singlehandedly squeeze all profit out of the hotel market, while challenging in the property rental sphere too.

6) Working with an agency: the boutique option

An agency is undoubtedly small fry when compared to the reach of the monster booking portals like Airbnb, VRBO and Booking.com. And that's the beauty of them. They can offer a finely honed package to the clientele that regularly books in your city, and offer a uniquely personal touch when dealing with guests and host alike.

Some agencies will use one of the big portals to help with their advertising of all of their portfolio. It's more common than you might think. Others will stand alone on their reputation, use of social media and print advertising in airline magazines and newspaper travel sections. Some might combine all options available to them to bring in bookings. Pebbles, an agency that is managed by one of the authors of this book, does something similar.

We're well aware that you're reading this knowing that one of the authors of this book might have a bias towards the benefits of using an agency. You'd be right. Simply put: An agency works on commission so only gets paid when you get paid. They also live or die by their reputation, so they have a big incentive to keep their property portfolio well maintained and brilliantly marketed. They are also responsible for your property even when it's not occupied by a paying guest.

The biggest advantage of an agency is its collective reputation. Web portals are not reviewed; they have an enviable lack of responsibility. Responsibility always rests with the host and the guest. The individual property reviews only go so far.

Listing your property with a reputable agency should buy you high visibility in a crowded space. Your rental space can feed from an already established reputation. This might mean that guests are prepared to pay a little more. Agencies also make the milking of your asset extremely easy. If you don't want to clean up after your guest, worry about a missing bathplug or liaise with a disgruntled customer it might be the avenue for you.

In return, agencies often demand a lot more from you prior to listing. They also usually want full control and may even limit your personal use. Their stipulations might not be right for your space. Budget offerings do not necessarily need uniformly fluffy white towels and toiletries – they need cheaper prices. Your space will become more clinical and less like your venture. This doesn't suit micromanagers who like to be involved.

And finally, beware of new agencies unless your location is small or you can tell they have a good reputation and reach. Many operate in the world's sunniest locations like Rio, Brazil or Hainan Island, China. Their staff and owners alike might rather be sitting on the beach than scrubbing your shower stall.

In short: Agencies are for you if your space is at the top tier of the market sector and if you prefer a hands off approach. Good agencies are also selective about what they take on, so it's sometimes less about you choosing them, and more them choosing you.

One final note: Doing it yourself is great when every penny counts or where your space is modest. If your overall income of estimated property earnings, plus any salary or dividends, leans towards a higher tax bracket, think carefully. Agency costs are tax deductible. Conversely, the government doesn't give tax breaks for the time you take to snap photos, write a property description then upload it to your web rental property.

When weighing up to agent or not to agent, consider how many hours you think you are going to put into the venture, and whether you have the time to devote to answering enquiries promptly. Make sure you're happy with the estimated hourly rate you'll be putting in, after any tax.

Looking after the guests is a whole new ballgame. There are emails to answer, dates to plug in, deals to negotiate and disgruntled guests to placate. An agency will solve damage disputes, credit cards payments and bizarre requests (from cots for triplets to alcohol-free cleaning products for a high allergy guest) on your behalf.

Is using a web rental portal or an agency best for you? The next 200 words should make that decision clear.

7) The world's shortest quiz – agency or booking website?

Still confused? Answer these five quick fire questions. Your answers will push your towards an agency or a short term accommodation website.

1) Is my property exceptionally fancy and fairly expensive?

2) Is my time to snap photos, write property descriptions, manage guests and sort through bookings extremely limited?

3) When I google 'holiday apartments in my city' does a reputable looking agency come up on the first page?

4) Do I keep losing items on my computer desktop and don't know the difference between a .jpg and a .gif?

5) Am I so rich that I could earn more in a day in my office than I could in a week fiddling around with Airbnb?

If mostly 'yes' well done. Your fancy property is probably best marketed by an agency who can take the effort out of advertising and ensure the right sort of clients come your way.

If mostly 'no' then congratulations are also in order. You'll keep more money your money by popping a free posting on VRBO or similar, and will still be able to control who books your place.

8) What to write on your apartment booking page

The photos you upload to your property profile may tell a thousand words, but it's the small print that will land the booking.

It's a tricky gig. At least there are a few don'ts that we can run through first.

As much as they may admire Dostoevsky, your potential renters aren't looking for War and Peace. They will routinely have five different property profiles open on their laptop at once, perhaps several on VRBO and another on HolidayLettings. They need the info about your property sharpish.

English is frequently a second language. If you're welcoming Chilean, Turkish or Chinese guests, it's unlikely any of them will know what an 'epic' stereo or a 'wicked' mattress is. A 'Bluetooth' stereo or a '$2,000' mattress will be more easily comprehended.

Don't waffle. As much as you love your place, guests need to quickly compare number of bedrooms (do they all have en-suite?) and kitchen facilities (must you walk through to use the bathroom?). Lists are great: "our apartment includes linen, towels, Wi-Fi, beach towels, guidebooks, children's games, iPad and a library of books, but not parking which is charged at $15 per day."

Put yourself in the shoes of your prospective guest and note down the information they would quickly like to acquire. If you're renting a property near Paris' Charles de Gaulle airport, talk up terminal access, parking options and proximity to Disney Land. If your container home is child-friendly state why: "our 60m2 space has a separate kids' play area, three boxes of games, PlayStation 4, two entirely separate children's beds with closed door access to parents' room and night light, plus kids' cutlery and plates." You get the picture.

On all property rental listings, the opening headline is the hardest to get right. Can you fit all your accoutrements on one 50-character line?

Here are examples of what not to write. All three exist in the real world and all lack inspiration:

"1 bedroom house near Paris"

"Private room in Ho Chi Minh City"

"Accommodation in Cape Town"

Pulse-raising huh? They really sprinkle your post-work holiday search with stardust.

Here are better examples based on those three:

"Cosy French cottage 30mins from Airport & Disneyland"

"Contemporary studio near cafés, bakeries and market"

"Luxurious sea view villa with hot tub"

As you can see, there's no need to mention Paris, Saigon or Cape Town in the description. Your guest is quite conscious of the city he or she is searching in.

Although the above isn't rocket science, if you have a friend who works in marketing get him or her to look over the copy. If not, get another friend to at least proofread what you've written. In short, be brief. Sell what's best about the space.

9) The dearest wishes of the richest generation in history

One of the biggest global travel trends is the 'Grey Getaway'. This is where retirees, exhausted by babysitting their grandkids for the holidays, depart on mass for sunnier climes. This massive movement has extended the reservation season for up to a month in many destinations.

The Western World's baby boom generation – people born in the post-war lovemaking fiesta between 1946-64 – hold a disproportionately large amount of global wealth. Some say these people benefitted from jobs for life. Younger generations look with envy at their generous pensions that kicked in age 60 or so.

Either way, it doesn't pay to ignore the wealth of this golden generation. Statistically, the sheer numbers are immense. The baby boom generation represents nearly 20% of the American public. In Britain, one in six people are now retired.

Combine these figures with no mortgages, no school fees and near unlimited holiday time, and you have recipe for success.

France's Cote d'Azur's region shows a similar picture to the global one. The tourist industry isn't focussed on families (these make up 16% of annual visitors). Nor is it all about backpackers (just 10% of incoming tourists are under 25). Instead, tourism chiefs are focussing on the 'Silver Dollar'. According to official figures, seniors aged 60 or over make up a mammoth 23% of French Riviera tourists.

How to take advantage of this growing market?

To glean these five tips, we asked our mothers and fathers, mothers-in-law and fathers-in-law, plus a dozen other 60- and 70-year-olds like themselves.

1) Make your apartment look cleaner than a hospital ward. This is where Airbnb fails as many of their holiday rental options look like student digs. A professionally staged photo shoot will deliver more bookings.

2) Offer your visitors flexible payment options. Most retirees prefer the security of a credit card. But some (like one of the authors of this book's father who has time to sit on eBay for several days at a time) prefers PayPal. Many opt for a bank transfer. And others (OMG!) write cheques like it's the 1990s. As much as you may loathe the latter, it's their call.

3) Liaise by phone. One of this book's authors reserves at least six holiday rental apartments for work or leisure each year. Being able to instantly book accommodation via credit card is ideal. Not for his parents. They distrust technology and prefer a call or a long email trail prior to booking. Let them.

4) Easy access. Elevator. A map of local stores. Properties within walking distance of tram/train/airport bus. All of these options score highly on the senior relative radar, according to the retirees we consulted.

5) Plentiful bathrooms. Don't ask me why, but when one of the authors' mother-in-laws books a place this becomes more important than Wi-Fi.

10) The dearest wishes of the generation who actually call the shots

Both authors of this book have kids. Both adhere to the saying: "A happy child is a happy family." When the vast majority of parents book a holiday home, it's the kids' facilities that's sell it.

What do those ankle biters demand that solace-seeking parents are all too happy to pay for?

Invest in a decent TV on the wall. Buy a $300 games console from Amazon. If you can, dedicate a room where grown-ups can deposit their kids then get some peace. If you do make these special dispensations, you can also market on kid-friendly websites like Baby Friendly Boltholes or Kid&Coe. We have seen great tree house effects made from funky IKEA bunk-beds with a small TV for each bunk.

In our experience families who have been happy with their accommodation often book again. At the Pebbles agency the record repeat custom for families is 11 successive visits. After all, if you can guarantee happy family holidays, why look elsewhere? At coffee mornings, school gates and play dates, these parents also tell others.

Even if you only have one space to rent, a property may hold its own if you pay for Google AdWords for exactly that hit. For example, "baby friendly accommodation in Marrakech" or wherever your property is located. A year or two down the line, with some repeat customers, we bet you'd hardly have to advertise again. If you're lucky enough to live near an attraction like Cedar Point in Ohio, Alton Towers in Staffordshire or Universal Studios in Singapore, a few sponsored AdWords may bring in all the bookings you need.

Insider tip. Get Netflix. Arrested Development, The Crown and dozens of kids shows – all for around $10 a month or the local currency equivalent – provides a marketing boon.

11) Telling the world

When marketing your apartment every little helps. Don't be afraid to tell everyone and his mother on Facebook that you have a nakamurake wooden hut for rent in Okinawa, Japan. Put a free advert in your local supermarket. Get your partner to tell her friends at the local sailing club. Invite your yoga buddies, dog walking group or coffee circle to look at the photos on your iPad.

Chapter 6 written in stone

1) The market for holiday letting websites is very muddy. Try Googling 'spare room for rent in Cartagena' or whatever property you intend to advertise to see what comes up.

2) Airbnb is a household name that offers free advertisements for properties as diverse as a gypsy wagon in Colorado, a lighthouse in Croatia or a ranch in Costa Rica. You'd be a fool not to check out what's for rent in your neighbourhood at the very least.

3) HolidayLettings from TripAdvisor are tricky to work with but offer massive exposure and are growing fast.

4) In property website terms, VRBO and its manifold brands have been around since the dawn of time. It never fails to do well, although its charges are high.

5) Booking.com will push your hotel style accommodation harder than a rented hire car. Its clientele is frequently price-led – make of that what you will. When starting your own short term letting revolution we advise advertising on more than one property portal to see which one suits you.

6) In your local short term letting agency has full booking calendars and a good reputation – and you have a unique place to market – contact them first. Working with an agency takes the sting out of almost every facet of property rental and pays dividends to those too busy to manage an asset themselves.

7) If you are so rich that you have a secretary to read your emails to you, you probably don't have time to become enmeshed in several apartment booking websites. Your property is also, probably, really, really, really nice. Use an agency to market it instead.

8) Put yourselves in the shoes of your guest. When you write your home listing, give an idea of which amenities/shops/theme parks are close and what family friendly additions/facilities/kitchen additions make your place unique.

9) Retired classes across Europe, Asia and the United States are the richest in history. Their needs cannot be overlooked if you intend to successfully market your property to a wide audience.

10) Parents book holiday homes that will keep their children happy. We know, as we do it ourselves.

11) If you want to make money, don't be shy. Tell everyone from your grandson's neighbour to your dog walker's daschund that you have a villa to rent in Penang, Malaysia.

Chapter 7: Expertly honing your asset

"I'm selling up and buying four new short term rental apartments across Asia and South America."

> "An investment in knowledge pays the best interest."
> **Benjamin Franklin**

Jasper Ribbers describes himself as a 'digital nomad'. This new class of entrepreneurs, aged 18 to 80, swan around the world without fixed abode, consulting via Skype as they travel.

"When I packed in my finance job in 2010 I only met a few people like me," says the young Dutchman. That situation has changed. In 2016 Ribbers lectured at Bangkok's Digital Nomad conference on the ecosystem that now supports his growing breed. Like co-working spaces and productivity apps. Plus outsourcing websites where mobile magnates such as himself can market their expertise to big Western firms while they sip coffee in Colombia or Kenya.

Ribbers' unique skillset revolves around a key growth market: teaching how better to market your property in the short term letting industry.

Each Friday morning, he hosts a live Facebook video feed where users chime in with questions about pricing strategies and investment cities. His recent blog posts profile new apps like Payfully, which allow property hosts to receive money from their bookings in advance, and Hostfully which makes a personal guidebook for your city. He also owns a YouTube 'how-to' series and a podcast library.

He then further monetises his skills by selling expert letting lectures and offering one-to-one coaching to make your property profile shine. Not to mention his best-selling Amazon guidebook, *Get Paid For Your Pad*. His salary is somewhere north of €100,000 per year. Which goes a long way in Saigon where he answered our WhatsApp call.

This incredible story started in Amsterdam, the Netherlands, and was only made possible by the advent of the web rental portals we now regard as commonplace. Five years ago Ribbers' only asset was a heavily mortgaged apartment in the edgy suburb of De Pijp. "I wanted to travel but there were three reasons I didn't want to rent my property long term," he recalls. "First, it didn't seem very lucrative. Second, I couldn't stay in my own home when I returned. Third, in Holland it's very difficult to remove a tenant if they overstay their contract."

Then came Wimdu, Airbnb and a host of short term letting websites with which Ribbers experimented. His financial background allowed him to fine-tune pricing. Single day stays proved unprofitable as his cleaning costs were high; raising prices during Amsterdam's King's Day street festival helped the bottom line. All new hosts go through similar periods of tinkering, fine tuning and introspection as their hone their skills month-by-month, year-on-year.

Ribbers' €150-per-night property now has 250 glowing reviews and nets over €50,000 per year. It's listed on the first page of Amsterdam's Airbnb portal.

"Of course there's now an entire industry built around this multi-billion-dollar market," he explains. The market that readers of this book will enter is literally that big. "Take revenue tools websites like Beyond Pricing and automatic online messaging tools like AvivaIQ. You Google what you need and can be sure it exists."

Ribbers offers three key rental recommendations for first-timers. The big one is photos. "Online viewers have a ludicrously short attention span. If the first image doesn't sell your USP, it's pretty much game over."

Second is communication. "People trust a hotel reservation. You can walk in to a physical building you know is there. So with an online property enquiry you must quickly reply with your guidebook and arrival tips to convince a guest that this amazing opportunity truly exists."

Third and final is pricing. "You'd be amazed how many hosts simply charge the same nightly fee all year long," says Ribbers. "It's galling to think they are missing serious money by not charging more in summer, or are missing bookings by not adapting to low season demand."

Does Ribbers see any clouds on the horizon? "Only opportunities," says the Dutchman. "Like some other Western cities, Amsterdam is starting to enforce its 60-day maximum rental rule for short term lets. So I'm selling up and buying four new short term rental apartments across Asia and South America."

He flies to Santiago in Chile this Thursday. We wish him luck.

Chapter 8: Smart but simple money multipliers

"Each time my friend's aunt stays in her Spanish villa she loses €4,000 in rental income. That's €40,000 over the last decade."

"Many receive advice, only the wise profit from it."

Harper Lee

In 1992, two management consultancy boffins from McKinsey and Company published a study in the Harvard Business Review. The duo looked at the pricing economics of 2,463 companies. They found that getting the price right for a product – be it a holiday home in July or a frozen turkey at Christmas – can increase profits by 11% assuming no changes in supply or demand.

Imagine that you earn €20,000 each year from your rental property. Why not get the price right and pay yourself another 11% more? That's €2,200 to be exact.

In our experience, which is pretty vast, most property owners don't bother to amend their prices according to season. In the American idiom they're hanging loose. In the British idiom they can't be arsed.

And who can blame them? If you start renting out your attic on a rental website or pimping your holiday home through a lettings agency, you should suddenly come into a lot of money that you didn't initially foresee. So why try harder?

Let's put it another way. In this chapter we showed a friend how she was losing €4,000 in rental income each year through one silly mistake. That's €40,000 over the past decade. If someone offered to top up your bank account by such a figure would you say no? Well then. Read on.

Of course, we don't want to raise your holiday rental profits by 11% a year. Oh no. We want to push them into outer space.

1) How to squeeze more from your 12-month rental calendar

Every rental property, from a campervan to a portfolio of holiday apartments, offers differing yields throughout the year.

In Moscow, Russia, the peak month is May (you gotta love those heavy weaponry processions through Red Square).

Come Christmas, a villa in Phuket, Thailand is gobbled up quicker than a steaming plate of Pad Thai.

What 12-month strategy should you use for your Mongolian yurt or Argentinian estancia? Grab a paper and pencil and we'll tell you.

Visit the tourist office where your property is located. Check the Internet for every local festival, business meetup and county show. Ask locals when the wedding season is. Log onto your Hilton Hotel – or local equivalent – and see what nightly charges they have set for a year in advance. Believe me, their hotel price calendar will have more ups and downs than Donald Trump's presidency.

Then print out your own rental calendar from 2014, 2015 and 2016 if you have them. Did clients book early for the months of April, August and December? When was your peak demand highest? What were your weakest months? Leave no stone unturned as you built up a complex picture of who books what and when. To re-quote Benjamin Franklin: "An investment in knowledge pays the best interest."

The final trick is to turn your knowledge into hard cash. Add between 50% and 75% to your prices in your peak month. Keep premiums high in your shoulder months. Keep family away from your spare room near the school holidays or Christmas ski season.

In short, no-one in your city, town, resort or island will have amassed as much rental calendar knowledge as you. Treat each month as a hard-won challenge to milk your property for as much as it's worth. Revel in breaking your year-on-year record every 12 months. Then treat yourself. Truly, just enjoy spending the cash.

2) Fixed costs versus variable costs

This is the simplest and most beautiful lesson in economics. The more you sell, the more you make.

The lesson is a tiny bit complex so we'll use an example to explain.

Every business in the world, from giant American grocer Walmart to your humble spare bedroom renter, has fixed costs and variable costs.

Fixed costs are the ones that stay the same no matter how many units you sell. In Walmart's case, they are heating, lighting, advertising and all the rest. If the company manage to sell just one Bluetooth speaker a year in all of its 12,000 stores, or sells millions of Bluetooth speakers, these costs stay exactly the same. All clear?

Let's pretend Walmart's fixed costs are a 10 million dollars per year.

Variable costs are ones that rise in comparison to each unit the business sells. For example, if Walmart sell only one Bluetooth speaker per year, the company will pay for one imported speaker from China, one grocery bag, one roll of gift wrap and all the rest. All still clear?

Let's pretend Walmart's variable costs per each Bluetooth speaker sold are $10 per item.

So, if you follow our example, if Walmart sell just one Bluetooth speakers it will cost the company $10,000,010. A fortune.

But if they sell two Bluetooth speakers the fixed costs don't rise. Once you've paid to heat, light and staff your 12,000 stores it costs no more to sell another piece of electronic hardware. Only variable costs rise, in this case by $10 per Bluetooth speaker.

So if Walmart sell 200 Bluetooth speakers it will cost the company $10,002,000. That cost per sale is $50,010 – still ludicrously expensive – but the figure falls the more you sell.

What if Walmart sell 20 million Bluetooth speakers per year? Now you're talking. The fixed costs don't change at $10,000,000. Variable costs are 20 million times $10, so $200,000,000 in all, making a grand total of $210,000,000. The cost per unit would thus be $10.50. Think of the profits that can be made selling Bluetooth speakers at that price.

This 'pack-em-high-sell-em-cheap' strategy has a proper economic name. It's called Economies of Scale. Walmart is a specialist in this.

In fact, the company welcome one hundred million people into their 12,000 stores every single week. Many of its supercentres are open 24 hours a day. By selling in such quantities, the company gleans as much as 8 cents from every dollar spent in the United States.

If Walmart were a country, it would have the twentieth-largest GDP in the world. That's bigger than Saudi Arabia, Sweden or Switzerland.

3) How Economies of Scale can make you more money

Amandine is a petite house near Antibes, France. It has a sun-soaked outdoor terrace and two sumptuous bedrooms upstairs. It rents for an average of €1,500 per week.

The properties fixed costs are quite high. Each year the owner, a Dutch lady called Sheila, pays €3,000 in local taxes, €1,000 in water bills and €1,000 for insurance. This figure of €5,000 stays the same no matter how many times Sheila rents her property throughout the year.

Variable costs – again, these are the extra costs Sheila bears for every rental week – are around €200. For each guest she buys a welcome pack stuffed with Provençal products, a lavender soap and a French baguette and local jam. She also pays for extra heating, general wear and tear, plus a cleaner to tidy up afterwards.

So, if Sheila rents Amandine for 10 weeks per year, the costs she pays per annum are €5,000 of fixed costs plus €2,000 of variable costs, giving her a grand total of €7,000. Her revenues for 10 weeks of rental are €15,000. That makes Sheila's total profit of €8,000, or just €800 per week. Not bad, but not brilliant.

But what if Sheila rents for longer? She certainly can, as Amandine is an adorable little place.

At 20 weeks of rental per year Sheila's variable costs are €4,000. But fixed costs are still €5,000, making €9,000 in total costs. At revenues of €30,000 she will make €21,000 in profit, or €1,050 per week. That's more like it.

Are we all clear that the more weeks Sheila rents out her property, the more money she makes per week? What a happy equation! I wish we'd learnt that at school.

One more time if you please. Now what if Sheila goes totally nuts? What if she never visits her adorable holiday property, gets dozens of repeat customers and rents Amandine like a maniac for 40 weeks per year?

Her variable costs will then be €8,000, plus unchanged fixed costs of €5,000, so €13,000 in total. Revenues for 40-weeks rental will be €60,000. That makes a profit of €47,000 or a massive €1,175 per week. That's real Economies of Scale. Sheila becomes the Walmart of short term holiday letting and lives happily ever after.

4) Why 100 people we've dealt with choose to limit the money they make

We've heard some great excuses over the years. For some people, cutting down their rental calendar to a minimum of weeks somehow sounds like a good idea. Consider these statements below.

1) "I don't want to rent my villa in Queensland, Australia for more than ten weeks a year in case it gets trashed."

2) "I only like to rent our Berlin, Germany apartment in summer because the heating bill costs a fortune."

3) "I'm not renting my place in France for any more weeks because I don't want to pay any more tax."

4) "If I get 20 weeks' rental per year for my Californian house I'm happy as that covers my mortgage."

5) "My place is worth £1,000 a week and it's not worth renting it for less. If I rent it for less, I'll get budget people who smell and won't look after the place".

Let's smash these myths once and for all. After all – as we've seen – the more you rent, the more you make.

1) We know of no rental properties that have been 'trashed'. Most property agencies charge a damage waiver (as seen in Chapter 4) and many owners add a waiver on VRBO, Airbnb or similar. It's a cinch to do. Moreover, the sort of clients who can afford a ski chalet in St Moritz or a pricey apartment in London are not the sort of clients who would trash it. People trash hostels, but not £250 per night *pied-à-terres* where they have left a digital trail including their passport, credit card and postal address enmeshed in their booking. If your property is trashed, then we're sorry. But allowing ten weeks of rental, not 40 weeks of rental, won't alter the probability of such a random event very much.

2) Your heating bill in Berlin won't break the bank if your apartment is rented in December. Yes, guests will use more hot water, lighting and heating in winter. But this sum won't be greater than your weekly rental income. If it was, then the entire German nation would go bankrupt.

3) The old 'not renting your property in case I pay too much tax' idea. It's like saying 'I don't want a pay rise because I'll only have to pay more tax'. The phrase is a well-used excuse for not getting your property on the market in the first place. As in the above example, you may pay more local taxes if you rent your property for a longer period. But this sum is extremely unlikely to be greater than your weekly rental income. If it was, then the entire French nation would pay more in tax than they earn. They don't (it just seems like that sometimes).

4) So 20 weeks of rental income pay for your Californian holiday home? Bravo! How much is that by the way? $8,000? $16,000? $32,000? If you're not using your holiday home those other 32 weeks per year, why not treat yourself and double your income by renting for 40 weeks instead of 20? (If you don't need the money then our address is on the cover of this book. Thanks!)

5) Says who? Your rental space is never worth what you think it is. It is worth what someone is willing to pay. If you've done your homework and it seems to be worth £1,000 you might attain that figure most of the time. Are you really going to give up 10 bookings at £900, that's £9,000 per year, when the right price doesn't come through? People who pay a little less do not smell any worse than a higher paying guest, and may smell much better. In fact, guests who feel they got a good deal are far more likely to look after your space than a guest who think they paid too much.

5) How the greatest lesson in economics can make you more money

Are you ready for a lesson in Opportunity Cost economics? You may rather be relaxing with a glass of rosé. But we urge you to read on. Because if you utilise this key economic concept, you will squeeze thousands more out of your rental property, holiday home or garden shed. Each and every year. That's a lot of glasses of rosé.

Opportunity Cost is the value of the alternative option forgone. For example, imagine you only had €2 in your pocket. With that shiny coin you could either purchase a glass of rosé in a pavement café, or ride the bus back home. With just €2 you can't afford both.

Therefore, the Opportunity Cost of drinking a glass of rosé is the fact that you have a 30-minute hike home. Easy so far? Now comes the lucrative bit.

Let's pretend you're the owner of a holiday home in Mallorca, Spain. You hope to holiday in your apartment for a week this August. Who wouldn't? The sun will shine. Clothing store Zara will have a summer sale. And you can sip Spanish rosé for €2 a glass.

But that week in the sun will cost you. How much? The Opportunity Cost of using your own holiday apartment this August is the amount for which you could have rented it.

That sunny week in Mallorca would therefore cost you €1,000, €2,000 or the equivalent amount of your weekly rental charge. That's what you would have had in the bank if you'd have stayed at home.

How can this miserly economic theory make me more cash?

It's obvious. The more you are absent from your property, the more money you make. Yet you'd be surprised how few property owners take heed of this information. So listen up.

If you own a second home, don't visit in peak season. If you rent out your primary home, stay away for six weeks in summer not just three. If you have a spare room, make sure it's not filled with old televisions that will never work again, books that are never read, or DVDs that you have no possibility of ever watching on your super-slim laptop. That said, if you can afford to fill an entire spare room with junk perhaps don't need to read this book.

Whatever you do, don't start gifting weeks in your holiday apartment to family and friends. Unless you're exceptionally generous. To use our favourite example, a friend offers her aunt two weeks in her villa in the Canary Islands, also in Spain, each Christmas. That's very generous, but she hasn't taken into account Opportunity Cost.

Each time her aunt stays for two weeks, she loses €4,000 in rental income. Every year. Or €40,000 over the last decade. Again, if you can afford to give your beloved aunt €40,000 directly from your bank account, you really don't need to read this book.

Last year we explained the concept of Opportunity Cost to this property owner. Oops! Now the poor aunt has to scrabble around for a hotel on Lastminute.com instead. But the owner has a lot more money for rosé. Around 2,000 glasses each year to be exact. Or 20,000 over the coming decade.

6) Why repeat customers are the best customers

Repeat customers are the best customers because they show up and pay up without any effort on your behalf. In our experience, repeat customers treat your apartment, treehouse or chalet as if it were their own. That means they take care of it, and tell their friends about "my pal's place we always visit in India, Finland or Peru".

How can you snag repeat custom? Or, to put it another way, how can you invite easy money to knock on your front door?

Offering a nice property with exemplary service is the obvious answer. Do you have enough plates, knives, forks, chairs, napkins and glasses for your potential eight guests as per your advertisement? Does your cleaner check for dust under each bed, cabinet and dresser? Do you pay your Meet & Greet guy an extra $10 to buy fresh croissants and a bunch of flowers for each guest? Penny pinching wins no pals. Instead, who cares wins.

We digress, but similarly, one of the authors' dentists cares deeply about him. So much so that she calls him every six months to schedule an appointment. He'd forget otherwise. Sometimes she tells him about a special offer for loyal customers on whitening, crowns or some such treatment. Guess what car she drives? An Audi R8.

Few people we interviewed love their clients like the dentist does. Even fewer email their previous guests each year. It's like they don't care about them. Poor previous guests...

One of our interviewees, Stuart, does care. His property in Capri on Italy's Bay of Naples rents well each summer. "So I email the former customers around Christmas," says Stuart, "as that's when most families plan their summer break." Stuart knows that fact because his family also do their planning over the Christmas break. He's put himself in his guests' shoes.

Clever Stuart also makes his guests feel loved. "I email them to say that whatever customers asked for last year, I've purchased, like a €200 BOSE stereo or new snorkelling kit." How kind is this guy?

Stuart also offers them a Christmas present. "I say that because they are loyal customers I'd like to give them 10% off if they book directly with me and not through a property rental portal like HomeAway." Of course for Stuart this isn't giving away much at all. He's saved the 10% commission he would have otherwise spent on advertising his place online.

Booking.com, the world's largest hotel booking engine, does something similar. They offer 10% hotel discounts to 'Genius' members, who are simply people who have booked before. The authors of this book are both Genius members so they often use Booking.com when looking for a hotel for a single night. The hotel booking website also calls any previous customers a 'Genius', which is a nice touch.

That's not all. Booking.com have another sneaky customer retention trick. On their hotel website they tell you when that accommodation option was last booked, and how many rooms are left.

As ever, Stuart is one step ahead. "In my Christmas email I also explain that I have three weeks left in July and only one in August or whatever. It's free marketing and it always gets a few bookings". Happy customers. Happy man.

7) Knowing when your customers book

When do your guests book your property? Well, in any business it pays to put yourself in your customers' shoes.

An American family booking summer vacation in the Czech capital of Prague will probably book about eight months in advance. It takes that long to rouse the family into agreeing on a certain week, then a dozen fraught WhatsApp messages, phone calls and emails to sort out transatlantic flights.

An Australian couple booking a campervan trip to Queensland will probably book about two months in advance. With no family involved, they are flexible enough to go whenever the vehicle is available. The campgrounds they intend to visit won't book up solid, so there's no need to plan too far ahead.

In either case it would pay to contact these guests either eight, or two, months in advance depending on who regularly books your place. Let each party know you're still there. Offer them a bottle of Moravian wine (in Prague) or Bundaberg rum (in Queensland) on arrival.

More importantly, make sure you advertise your property in time. We deal with scores of owners who only register their Swiss ski chalet with a lettings agency in September, then hope to get bookings at Christmas. Not good business. In that instance you can kiss goodbye to all those Germans and Scandinavians who plan a year in advance.

Similarly, we meet clients who block off parts of their booking calendar as they half expect to use their property for one of those weeks. Don't do it. Fit around your high paying guests instead.

Here's the bottom line. If you are open for bookings for 52 weeks per year, and advertise a year in advance, you will do better than someone who open for bookings for 20 weeks per year, who advertises six months only in advance. Obvious, but true.

On a final note, properties which are more unique are more likely to be booked in advance than standard properties. This is because customers browsing months in advance fear missing out on such a rare place. However, they are confident of booking a hotel-style rental space at the last-minute as there are so many of these on the market. To boost rental enquiries, make your property more unique, perhaps with original artwork, access to a shared garden or a free city tour passes for each booking.

8) The final lesson of behavioural economics

Richard Thaler is a world leader in the field of behavioural economics. It's the theory that business decisions are affected by psychological, social or emotional factors. That means parting with money using your heart not your brain.

Early in Thaler's lecturing career he stumbled across an unlikely lesson. He set a purposely hard midterm exam peppered with tricky questions that would highlight all the missing nuggets of knowledge from the syllabus.

In Thaler's words: "The exam succeeded in my goal – there was a wild dispersion of scores – but when the students got their results there was uproar".

That's because the average score on Thaler's test paper was only 72 points out of 100. Or 72%. It made no difference to distribution of exam grades: those with the average score received a B, the top fixed percentage of papers received an A, a certain set percentage received a C so on. It's just that on exam papers set by other tutors any score over 65 would net a B, while if you pushed 80 points you could get an A. A score of 72 'seemed' low.

So what did Thaler do to appease the student revolt?

For the next exam he simply set the test out of 137 points, rather than out of 100 points. That way the average test score was in the 90s. His students were ecstatic.

Of course, it made no difference to the students' grades. The same top percentage received an A, the same middling percentage got a B. But the behavioural concept proved so successful that he set all his future tests out of 137. To quote Thaler from his book *Misbehaving: The Making of Behavioural Economics*: "To an economist, no one should be happier about a score of 96 out of 137 (70%) that 72 out of 100 (72%), but my students were".

What lessons do we learn from Thaler's students?

Firstly, no-one wants to be 'nickel-and-dimed', to use the American expression. Guests don't want to check-in with an obvious penny pincher. If visitors have to pay $20 extra for towels, a €45 deposit for linen and €7 a day to use the pool they become cheesed-off and turned-off. It's far more appealing to charge an all-inclusive price instead and tell guests how kind you are: "free use of 30ft (10m) swimming pool and luxury cotton beach towels".

Secondly, customers don't 'behave' in a rational economic way. When booking a hotel or buying a new watch, they like to 'think' they are getting a bargain. Your property may be far more expensive than most, but if you can justify its value with free theme park tickets (if you're near Universal Studios, California) or a complimentary case of wine (if you're in Tuscany, Italy) – or use of an iPad loaded with great movies – they will lap it up.

Chapter 8 written in stone

1) Plan your 12-month rental calendar as if you're organising a battle. Pretend you're Winston Churchill in his basement War Room. Raise your prices in your peak month – and don't use the property yourself during that time. The more meticulous your planning, the more money you will make.

2) Play like Walmart. The more items the world's biggest grocery store sells; the more profit they make from each item. Your property's fixed costs (insurance, advertising) stay the same no matter how long you rent it out. So it pays handsomely to rent for longer.

3) Economies of Scale mean the more weeks Sheila rents out her property, the more money she makes per week. What a happy equation! Please do the same.

4) Some owners voluntarily choose to limit how much money they make. Go figure. Don't be shy about how many weeks your rent out your place. There is absolutely no harm in being greedy. If you feel guilty about the extra cash in your account, make a sizeable donation to UNICEF.

5) Think about opportunity cost. The 'price' of staying a week in your property is the sum that you would otherwise gain by renting it out. If you rent your apartment, villa or garden shed for $2,500 per week, then you forgo $2,500 by simply staying there that week yourself. Put simply, the more you vacate your own property by holidaying with your mum/brother/daughter/uncle/ex-boyfriend, the more money you make.

6) Repeat customers are the best customers. It costs nothing extra to email them and offer them a discount for next year, thereby avoiding the booking fees charged by VRBO or Airbnb. If you truly love your guests, say it with flowers when they arrive.

7) Work out when most of your customers book. Then shout hello at this very moment. More importantly, make sure your booking calendar is open in case these guests want to book a year, or even two years, in advance. You would be shocked by how many owners are caught out by this.

8) All customers, including short term rental guests, 'behave' in uneconomic ways. For extravagant purchases, like spending on holidays, gadgets and Christmas treats, they're prepared to justify higher costs for something that makes them feel special. If you throw in free theme park tickets into your apartment booking you can potentially charge more than those vouchers are worth. Especially if you can buy bulk at a discount.

Chapter 9: The reviews that went wrong

"Come in and try the worst porridge that one woman on TripAdvisor had in her life."

> "Criticism may not be agreeable but it is necessary. It calls attention to an unhealthy state of things."
>
> **Winston Churchill**

Since 2000 TripAdvisor has notched up 435 million reviews. Many contributors purvey the loathsome spelling and execrable grammar associated with the portal.

Tripadvisaargh is a network that collates the most stupidly compelling TripAdvisor reviews of all time. Here are six of their best:

"In Edinburgh for few days and on the last day my wife I went in for lunch half way through the meal my wife started to choke she then pulled out of her mouth a large elastic band the staff seemed to think it was amusing." wayneo867

"My daughter, (13) saw 2 people on the sofa next the bar 'making love' whilst being videoed by the chef." A TripAdvisor user

"I was chatting to my partner when he said to me in a quiet tone, 'Look at the mirror.' I turned to see the mirror attached to an old dresser moving back and forth quite considerably on its own. We watched the ghostly occurrence for a few seconds until it became still." Jacqueline

"Beach is too sandy. It's a great beach, just too sandy." Tomgreene

"When we got there, my wife, Ebel, and I we unhappy to find the color of the (San Francisco Golden Gate) bridge was not exactly as it was in all the photos in all the advertisings." Elmeryethel

"We had a good meal at the private function then entered the bar where we were met by the rudest staff member I have ever come across. We said to her booked five bedrooms and spent a lot of money. Her response was, "what do you want, a medal?" A TripAdvisor user

Alas, the subject of our next chapter is a serious one. With nearly 400m monthly users (a total greater than the populations of the USA and United Kingdom combined) TripAdvisor rightly claims to be the world's largest travel site. It owns web portals as diverse as ocean liner message board Cruise Critic and airline seat monitor SeatGuru. Plus a massive short term letting portal, HolidayLettings.

In the early days, sites like TripAdvisor and Yelp positioned themselves as a caring and sharing community of like-minded people giving credit to small businesses trying hard to please. In recent years they've shown up the darker side of consumer contributions. Modern society and technology encourages us to rate everything we buy and everything we consume. Lost in this globalised world, sometimes referred to as the 'age of rage', we can lose our natural empathy with the human being on the receiving end of any rant or moan.

That there are no consequences for the reviewer, often left anonymously, is part of the problem. That's why some owners are fighting back.

Like Arlo Calderbank, the manager of the Nook Neighbourhood Café in Stockport, England. This cute café has notched up 100-plus five star reviews between Google and TripAdvisor since it opened just a few years ago. Calderbank's ire was raised over TripAdvisor comments concerning both his menu and the size of his cosy café. Each morning the Englishman wheels out a chalkboard and uses it at every opportunity to write something different and poke fun at a recent review. Like these three:

"Come into our cafe that Gary from TripAdvisor said was 'small and cramped'. We're called Nook for a reason Gary."

"Come in and try the worst porridge that one woman on TripAdvisor had in her life."

"Tastes nothing like Costa. Meant as a complaint, taken as a compliment".

Calderbank's ripostes have gone viral. They touched a nerve with multi-generational population that scours reviews before booking a holiday, purchasing a TV, choosing a children's school or buying a book on Amazon.

Things are changing in the social media scene too. In Beijing a five-year digital roll out by the Chinese government began this year. The aim is to allow people to "know each other better" by a social credit score based on their online interactions. Yes, it could all be a government ploy by the Communist Party of China. But it might not be long before personal ratings show on Facebook and LinkedIn. After all, who wants to be friends with a doubting sourpuss?

Uber allows for ratings of the patron as well as the driver. Airbnb allow hosts to review their guests. A study done by Boston university in 2015 was revealing. They compared reviews by TripAdvisor and Airbnb for the same products. Airbnb properties received higher rating scores by 14% when compared to TripAdvisor. By needing to keep their own rating high, the guests tended to be more complimentary about their hosts.

Before the next chapter talks about what to do in order not to receive a terrible review, we'll leave you with one final TripAdvisor gem:

"The meal was ruined by midgets (sic) everywhere, and we were sitting inside. We even moved tables but we were either followed by them or they were at that table too. We woke up the following morning covered in bites and very itchy." A TripAdvisor user

Chapter 10: Why your reviews need to go right

"Receiving a negative review is like coming down with flu. It's very rare. Just a royal pain in the ass."

"Publicity can be terrible. But only if you don't have any."
Jane Russell

WLaura is a top tier Level 6 TripAdvisor contributor from Bucharest, Romania. She sounds a touch crazy.

This is her two-star assessment of the Hotel Jean Moet in France's Champagne region from 2016:

"Bed is too small, linen are the cheapest, towels are disgusting. In bathroom one bulb was out of order, I asked to be changed and they told me a story about the fact that the owner himself has to do it... Yes, sure! Maybe the Pope from Rome!!!

"If you want breakfast you have to announce one day before? Hello?!!! I suppose because they do not want to spend a few more cents on food that is not consumed...at a 4 star hotel?!!...
Well, people come and go, Epernay is not the biggest attraction of France."

But the courteous TripAdvisor response from the hotel's receptionist, Mélissa, makes WLaura sound uniformed, untrusting and unworthy of opinion. Read on and you'll be smirking along with receptionist, not the disgruntled guest:

"We are sorry that you didn't have a great stay with us.

"About the bulb in the bathroom, that's absolutely not what I told you. I explained you that we need to be 2 person to change it (one who holds the mirror and one who changes the light). As I was alone at the reception, I couldn't do it. I'm sorry that you couldn't understand that.

"We asked you when you arrive if you want breakfast in the morning because it is easier for us to know in advance. If you really don't know, that's not a problem for us.

"I think you should try a 2 stars hotel in Epernay, and see that you won't have the same service, as we helped you for many things.

"Kind regards, Mélissa"

The moral? Don't get mad. Get even.

Mélissa's response also makes the reader think that the Hotel Jean Moet is a small, personable hotel that has been taken for a ride by a nasty character. And everybody loves the small guy. Which is just how you want a play a negative review.

We realise this sounds creepy, but WLaura's review really made us want to check her TripAdvisor profile.

To salve your curiosity, we can confirm that of WLaura's 215 TripAdvisor reviews 64 are 'Poor' (two stars) and 56 are 'Terrible' (one star). Sounds like just the sort of woman you'd like to invite for dinner.

1) Welcome to the world

Our entire universe is wrapped in reviews. You don't rent a movie on iTunes without scanning the customer star rating. You wouldn't join a gym without checking online opinions.

People's annual holidays are far more important than a rental movie and all the rest. It's when people splash out, spend quality time and plan the best break they possibly can.

We know of no one, young or old, who doesn't page up their prospective hotel on Trivago, check the customer ratings on HomeAway or regard the review score on Booking.com.

That's why this chapter will teach you how to glean as many five-star reviews as you can.

And how the occasional psycho review from hell – as it may happen to you – can be turned to your distinct advantage.

2) How to get a five-star review

Think about it. Why did you give that hotel or rental apartment a five-star review last summer?

It must have been a special place. When you checked in, it looked even better than the photos. There was a welcome bowl of fruit or a bottle of wine. Great linen. Great bed. It ticked all the boxes, just as your rental space should.

But when was the last time you *purposefully signed into a hotel or rental website* and spent two minutes reviewing a fabulous place you stayed in?

We'll bet you're a very busy person. And the only reason you wrote the review was because you were prompted. You received an email that said: "We're glad you had a super stay. It will really help us host more great guests like you if you spent two minutes writing a review. Here's the link: www.reviewmyplace.com."

Why would a previous visitor bother to "help you host more great guests"? Giving a review doesn't help them. Indeed, the visitor may prefer to keep your place a secret for as long as possible. So here's why: They will review your property because he or she likes you and wants to pass his or her thanks.

Rental properties are places where an owner can contact the guest in advance to ask if they need anything special.

Or be a telephone call away during their stay. What we're saying is, unlike corporate hotels, hosts can easily go the extra mile.

You can go the extra ten miles by querying your soon-to-arrive guest further. Do they need a beach recommendation, a list of activities for their kids or a map of the local allergy-free food stores in advance?

You can email or SMS your guests the morning after they arrive. Check all is well. Offer a restaurant tip. Be there for them. Then they will be far, far more likely to take the time to write a review for you when they return home. It's their thank you for your great service. Call it a 21st-century tip.

It's obvious. If you offered a fabulous rental experience, and kept in touch with your guests throughout, your follow-up email asking for a review will likely be answered.

The 'please review me' template below has worked wonders for dozens of friends and colleagues. To avoid negative feedback online (more of which later) note the sentence that asks the guest to send you any adverse comments directly, rather than posting them on the Internet.

"Dear Robert,

We're glad you had a fabulous time in Mexico City last week.

If you believe that our apartment warrants a 5-star review, we would love it if you shared your thoughts here: www.airbnb.com/review/property123

However, if you're holiday was not 100% perfect, could you reply to me directly to tell us exactly why? We are keen to act upon any feedback you have.

Best wishes, Miguel"

Tip. Have an amazing review you'd like your guests to see first? Take a screengrab of it (or get your techie daughter or silver surfing granny to make one if you're not sure how). Then post this screengrab with the other photos in your property profile.

3) Using your review response to sell your property twice over

Potential guests read reviews like the Pope reads the bible (and if you're reading this Holy Father, *buongiorno*). With solid reviews in place, these visitors will book your lighthouse, mobile home or two-bedroom condo more readily than your competitor around the corner.

Now comes a simple piece of lucrative advice that few in the property rental game follow.

Let us explain. After a visitor reviews your place you have the opportunity to post a response. Your paragraph of feedback then gets pasted in a very visible place just below the review.

It's here that you can use your response to sell your property twice over.

When replying to a review don't just scribble: "Thanks for the great review Robert come back to Mexico City soon ;-) !!!!"

That would be a cruel waste. Opt for the following instead:

"Robert, I'm so happy you enjoyed the market restaurants in Mercado Roma plus the bottle of Casa Madero wine we left you. We're also thrilled your children had a great time in the nearby Chapultepec Park. As do all our family guests - it's twice the size of New York's Central Park! We agree – the two bikes we leave for guests are lots of fun. Thanks to your feedback we will install child seats on both of them so other families can tour Mexico City's new bike lanes. You are welcome anytime! Miguel."

Miguel takes a minute to sell his place *twice over* in his response to each review. Miguel will therefore net more bookings than a similar apartment with no host feedback.

Obviously, your review response must vary each time to flag up location, amenities or whatever his unique selling point is. When you reply remind every potential guest about your proximity to the ski gondolier, the beach or the photogenic market. Tell them about your Bluetooth stereo, your smoothie blender or your Teppanyaki grill. Assure them your space is perfect for couples, solo travellers, families or business groups. Or foodies, culture vultures, skateboarders or surfers.

Your property's reviews and your responses to them will be read more times than the notes you write at the tail end of your property listing. Use them to sell yourself twice over.

4) Hitting reply all

You have to reply to all reviews. Only replying to the occasional bad ones will stain your personality as a touchy crackbrain.

Don't use a stock response either. The cut'n'paste job below is used to reply to *nearly all* the TripAdvisor customer postings by Stefania Catozzi who works at the Villa Glori Hotel in Rome, Italy:

"Dear Guest,

"We are glad to hear that we meet your expectations and that you enjoyed our nice hotel, comfort of the room, Breakfast, helpful staff. It is our goal to consistently provide customer satisfaction and your comments are very important to us.

"The feedback we receive from valued guests like yourself, enables us to keep up the good work. Once again, we appreciate you taking the time to share your comments with us and we hope to see you at Villa Glori Htl again in the future.

"With Kind regards, Stefania Catozzi"

Can you feel Stefania's magic here? What's that you say...Stefania obviously doesn't give a hoot? We're shocked.

(At least Stefania actually takes time to reply to her hotel's TripAdvisor postings, which many in hotels in Rome don't.)

Let's get something straight. When somebody is booking their business trip, let alone their only holiday of the year, they will reserve with the people who seem to care the most about their guests.

Leaving a considered response to a review also lets guests know that you really love them.

Hopefully your beloved visitors will be so touched that they book again. That's free marketing at its best. The Pebbles rental agency in Nice, France, sends personal emails of thanks to every reviewer. About 35% of the agency's business is repeat custom.

Writing a well thought-out reply – to reviews both good and bad – might also include flagging up what you plan to offer next year:

"Please revisit in 2018 when we will have converted the living room roof into a sun terrace with barbeque."

"When your family returns next year we will have installed a telescope to view the Northern Lights from the balcony upstairs."

Needless to say, the more you sell your property, the more you earn.

5) "Nothing is more vulgar than haste." Ralph Waldo Emerson

Receiving a negative review is like coming down with flu. It's very rare. There's seldom any cause. It's just a royal pain in the ass.

Our experience proves that most prime properties receive one shocking review for every 50 sublime ones. It won't hurt too much, and over time they still maintain a healthy review score.

Most of us don't read bad reviews as gospel. That's because we're not insane. We know that many negative netizens display their tantrums on the web where they think they'll have an audience since real people gave up listening a long time ago. We also know that the aggrieved or angry are itching to type before they've reached the departures lounge, while the rest of us sip cappuccinos near Duty Free. Most level-headed people either don't review at all, or review nicely and fairly.

As much as we believe this, like the flu, a bad write-up takes does take to overcome. It temporarily kicks you to the floor. But your response should never, never, *never* be written in haste.

If a bitchy two-star review pops up leave it for an hour. Calm down. Don't take it personally. Your gut instinct will be to right the injustice as soon as possible because you think the whole world is watching. They're not. As special as your space is, it's really not *that* important. If the one or two people that see this review overnight and choose not to book because of it, you probably don't want those people as guests anyway. Don't play into this reviewer's hands and join his toxicity. Be Zen. Gather the force. Prepare to strike back when you're good and ready.

Now, what goes on online stays online. Forever. If you sexted a semi-clothed photo to a high school sweetheart (classy guy that you undoubtedly are) that picture will still exist when your kids are in college. It's not a good look.

When you stab out an angry reply describing why your reviewer is TOTALLY WRONG about your rental space it will still be read in ten years' time.

History can't be deleted. It's easy to come across as a paranoid nutcase. Don't let it happen to you.

Instead, after your hour break, type up your response to the frosty review in Word or in an email body. There are several reasons for this. Firstly, bad grammar or spelling mistakes shows you've replied – like a psycho – in a blood-raising frenzy. Secondly, you can re-read your post an hour later to check you really want to send it. Thirdly, you can have a friend or partner look over your copy to double check you really *really* want to read what you just wrote in a decade's time.

Still happy with your text? Cut and paste your reply onto your property profile page. And remember. What goes on online stays online.

6) Speaking words of wisdom

When there really was a fault with your product, what should you write?

Firstly, thank the reviewer for bringing the broken washing machine or dust under the bed to your attention. Assure them you will fix the problem for all future guests (who may well read both the review and your reply to it).

Apologise. Sincerely. Sorry goes a long way. You're only human and cleaning mistakes or a broken appliance happen. Most people accept this. Show your human side, say how you've rectified the issue, and move on.

Secondly, tell your critic that you were overjoyed the rest of their vacation or business trip was a great success. Assure them they are welcome back anytime. Tell them that if you can help with anything else, you'd like to and perhaps they can email you personally?

What will a prospective punter think of you then? That you're a considerate host who slipped up through no fault of your own, and that you will make the property even nicer for future clients. Potential guests will forgive you – they only care about how the experience is going to be for their stay.

One final point. Notice how politicians rarely reply to the points a questioner has raised? They know that to talk about the point means it will remain tomorrow's news, and they want the news to move on to a more positive summit. It's a linguistic trick we can use too.

So don't answer every niggle the reviewer has raised in endless paragraphs. Writing a 500-word defence is not only too boring for guests to read. It makes your place look *really* bad. Instead answer a leading point the displeased guest has raised with friendly élan, then point out how you'll repair the issue this week.

7) What to do if your badmouthing reviewer is a whack-job

Believe us, there are some fruitcakes out there. Demoniac sociopaths who feel inexplicably stung by life and take it out not on a jogging track or in a yoga studio but on a keyboard. Their friends and enemies alike all live online. It's a sad existence.

If such a whack-job has vented their spleen on you, move on. Not forgiving someone is like letting them live rent free in your head for the rest of your life.

But you still have to answer their review.

The trick is to expose your bad-mouther as the raving lunatic, rather than yourself. The task is easier than it sounds. The French hotel example we gave you in the opening of this chapter is a good one to copy.

Answer the review with humour. Point out where the crank is mistaken, and why the claims he or she has made about your property or you are untrue. Explain that as their criticism is nonsensical you cannot help them any further. You can also tell the world that your previous 20 guests all awarded you a five-star review.

If a crazy reviewer actually threatens you, so much the better. Once they type "if you don't provide me with a refund in 24 hours I'm going to ruin your reputation on TripAdvisor", you have a case that you can take to court, or at least the rental website or review portal itself. The world may have moved on a bit, but under the true letter of the law, this is still blackmail and in many countries still carries a penal sentence.

A short answer is probably all you need to do to make them think twice about what they actually now post. For example, the Pebbles rental agency in Nice, France once received the following email:

"I'm coming to stay next week. I have already called about this, and you were dismissive. I am a blogger. I want a 50% deduction off my stay in return I'll write a great review for you. I do this a lot and I'm good at it. I've stayed with you once before so I'll miss out the crap service I thought I got last time if you give me the discount. I haven't yet written by experience on TripAdvisor. I'll wait to see how you respond first."

This guest had actually stayed with Pebbles three times before and each time he'd been over to the office to complain about something or other. Patience only stretches so far. Pebbles didn't really want him back; he was a royal pain. Yet he kept on coming.

Here was Pebbles reply:

"Thank you for your email. I'm sure you wrote this in haste and probably didn't mean to commit blackmail.

"However, due to the blackmail contained in your email, we're afraid we can't communicate further with you. Therefore, please do not expect a reply to any more communications you send.

"We're afraid that if this blackmail persists, we will have to give your correspondence to the police for them to take whatever action they consider appropriate.

"We hope you enjoyed your previous stays with us."

Not only did he not post anything on TripAdvisor, but he didn't communicate with Pebbles again.

Like blackmail, defamation or libel definitions vary state to state and from country to country, however the broad stroke definition is that someone has defamed you if they have written/said untruths about you/your property with malicious intention to do harm. Damages, in theory, can be substantial. In practice, it's probably better to warn the slanderer and move on. We bet there's little harm done except to your feelings for a day or two.

8) Playing 'the competition'

Occasionally a one-star review comes from a rival apartment owner or competitor rental agency. These people seek to damage your business in order to boost theirs. Fortunately, these evaluations are even easier to turn into a positive.

By way of example, Pebbles received a one-star Facebook review. It was from a Rebecca Martin and said simply "dreadful service, dreadful company – stay well clear".

This came as a big surprise as Pebbles don't get many bad reviews. And if they do, you can bet they have heard of the guest. The company checked their emails and bookings database. There was nothing of a Rebecca Martin anywhere. Here's how they answered:

"Hi Rebecca, thanks for taking the time to review. I'm sorry your experience wasn't up to expectations. If you'd like to give us more detailed feedback about where we could have done a better job, please send your thoughts to info@nicepebbles.com. Only with your feedback can we continue to build upon the service we provide. Kind regards, Pebbles."

This is the only way they could contact this purported guest. They waited. Nada.

Suspiciously, this Rebecca Martin had never left a review for any other company. By chance Pebbles discovered that a Rebecca Martin was a Facebook friend of one of their staff, Emily.

Emily had worked with her previously in a bar, but didn't really know Rebecca. What Emily did know is that Rebecca had connections with our competitors. Hmmm. Emily offered to private message her and wrote a longer version of the following:

"Hi Rebecca, we don't know each very well and it's certainly been a long time since we have had any contact. However, I am still living in Nice and working for Nice Pebbles, as I have been for almost five years. I am currently helping to improve their social media presence and have come across a bad review that you wrote back in 2015. I have looked into why you may have posted it but can't find a record of you staying with us. I'm wondering if you could tell me why you left it? I hope you're well, Emily."

Months later still nothing.

It's been two years since Rebecca Martin's review, who Pebbles now know wrote this post with far different intentions than to actually critique the service she received. Have the agency suffered? Not really. Does it hurt? Yes, a little. That she had to stoop this low says a lot more about her than the company she was attempting to review.

Pebbles recently posted this reply:

"Hi Rebecca, we take our reviews very seriously because we aim to provide the best possible service to all our guests. Since you left this review we've checked our database of 15,000 sets of guests, 99% of them happy with our service. There is no record of a Rebecca Martin ever staying with us, let alone being unhappy with our service.

"As we have attempted to email you and to contact you via social media with no response, we have concluded that this yours is a bogus review with the direct intention of harming out company."

The net outcome? We'd hope Pebbles look like a reputable agency that has been purposefully attacked by a keyboard coward. And when anybody Googles Rebecca Martin – be it for a job interview or a girlfriend background check – well, she might not get the job or the boy.

Remember, what goes online stays online.

Chapter 10 written in stone

1) You didn't buy this book without reading the reviews. You sure as hell wouldn't purchase something more important, like your annual holiday, without doing the same.

2) If your guests love both you and your apartment, they will take five minutes out of their busy lives to write a review. Your job? Put a ring on it.

3) Your response will live underneath every customer review about your rental space. It's prime real estate that every potential guest will see. Make it count.

4) Stefania at the Villa Glori Hotel doesn't seem to care. What sort of signal does that send about the rest of the hotel?

5) Don't respond to bad reviews in haste. It will make you look like a psycho. Forever.

6) Writing a rebuttal longer than War & Peace will only make your place look bad. Apologise if necessary, tell future guests how you will fix the problem, and move on.

7) There are serious crazies out there. Let them look like the raving lunatics they are, but don't become one yourself.

8) The Rebecca Martins of this world will stoop to giving you bad reviews to assist your competition. It's how you deal with these people that counts.

Chapter 11: When reviews become the market

"72% of TripAdvisor users would not consider booking a rental property that had zero reviews."

> "Truth is like the sun. You can shut it out for a time, but it ain't going away."
>
> **Elvis Presley**

We're sorry if the last chapter instilled a sense of fear. Reviews count for that much. So much so that many critique websites, like TripAdvisor, have launched their own rental portals, while traditional property booking sites, like VRBO/HomeAway, become ever focussed around guest feedback.

If you aren't convinced of this burgeoning market by now, regard the figures in the following two paragraphs.

TripAdvisor entered the vacation rentals business in 2008. It only had 50,000 listings. "Since then, we've seen tremendous organic growth and we've made several further acquisitions," says Laurel Greatrix, an associate director at TripAdvisor Rentals. These subsumed brands include HolidayLettings in 2010, Niumba in 2013, Vacation Home Rentals in 2014 and HouseTrip in 2016.

TripAdvisor Rentals, which also operates brands like FlipKey, has since grown its inventory to nearly a million properties in 190 counties.

"Rentals is a fast-growing part of the TripAdvisor business and the travel industry in general," says Greatrix. "A recent TripAdvisor survey showed that 67% of travellers planned to stay in a vacation rental in 2016 – up from 52% in 2014. More travellers than ever are seeing the great flexibility, amenities and value for money rentals offer." By being generally more expensive and infinitely more boring, hotels have lost their allure.

TripAdvisor and its rental minions are now carving a path for other rental portals to follow. In short, the travel industry is taking control of its 'wild' property leasing offshoot and consolidating it into a regular travel package. "You can book your vacation rental and then immediately book flights, restaurants or even local attractions, all without leaving our site," says Greatrix.

Since 2017 Airbnb have offered their guests the chance to book guided tours in conjunction with their holiday or business reservation. The rental apartment you're enticed to sign up to after reserving your easyJet flights is fulfilled by Booking.com. As far as TripAdvisor Rentals goes, Greatrix claims that "leveraging the wisdom of more than 400 million travel reviews" is her site's best marketing USP.

And finally, what's the burning question you always wanted to ask a TripAdvisor director? We'll guess it's how to deal with negative reviews.

"It's a subjective question," says Greatrix. "Good reviews are undeniably powerful and it gives users huge peace of mind that their vacation rental choice will live up to their expectations. In 2015 we undertook a survey that showed that 72% of users would not consider booking a rental property that had zero reviews."

Her advice on managing negative reviews is to tackle the points raised and use your right of reply to explain how these issues have been addressed. "If a homeowner does receive critical feedback, we encourage them to leave a response. Homeowners can respond to any review, thanking users for the positive comments and explaining and addressing the critical ones."

The all pervasive success of TripAdvisor proves how powerful reviews are. As if you didn't already know.

Chapter 12: The longer you rent, the more you earn

"Failure to show your rental manager where the water stopcock is can cause thousands in damages."

"A small leak will sink a great ship."

Benjamin Franklin

In Chapter 8 we discussed variable costs. In Chapter 10 we talked about property reviews. This chapter on wear and tear ties in with both of them.

On the negative side, the longer you rent, the more everyday costs arise, from decorating to purchasing new bed linen. On the upside, the longer you rent, the more money you accrue. The more your reputation and good reviews grow, the more repeat bookings you should achieve.

In short, the more you rent, the better you become at it. This enables you to fine tune your letting strategy to the tune of – in the case of many hosts we've spoken too – 10% extra income each year.

There's one more key factor to comprehend. It's certainly great earning €20,000 in your first year of letting. But what if you managed that sum every year for 10 years. Or 20 years. Or 30. That latter timeline would net you €600,000 over the course of your rental space's three-decade lifetime. Get that on-going investment right now and the retirement package of your dreams could await.

1) Can you accept the following?

This is a tough start to any chapter. Granted, it's not going to engage as readily as a sham marriage husband on a passport scam. But if you can accept the following factual sentences then you will make a great short term letting host over the coming decade. If you can't, then think twice about renting your lighthouse, villa or converted church.

- I'm delighted to be receiving an income from my rental property.

- I accept that I may not be able to use my property if a booking has come in before I have blocked off my own holiday dates.

- I recognise that I will probably have to put between 5% and 10% of my annual rental income back into the property for wear and tear and occasional irrecoverable damage.

- I understand that very occasionally I could be unlucky with a guest and may have to claim on my landlord insurance for damage, and I appreciate that this is part of the overall picture of renting my property.

- I know I will have to equip my rental space with an eye for what guests require rather than my own personal preferences.

- I'm OK with a few small ornaments or books going missing over time and accept that is part of renting to short-term guests. I accept that I'll just have to replace these items every couple of years and know that not all guests are the same.

- I accept that I might have to pay more for emergency repairs if a guest is shortly due to arrive at my property, because time is of the essence. My efforts will be repaid in the overall picture of a high annual rental return.

Which was the worst sentence for you? The 5% to 10% wear and tear per year one? Or the snaffling of your precious *objets d'art*? Well, get over it. Both are part and parcel of taking the short term letting rollercoaster. Ride it, or get off now.

2) Managing damage

As discussed in chapter 4, it pays to make your property as robust as humanly possible. This doesn't mean that your space can't have style. Nobody wants to rent an airport lounge.

Instead we're talking a high quality showerhead that won't leak. Tile floors in kitchen areas where spots of water can't cause damage. Carpets of the non-beige or non-sheepskin rug variety. Tiles grouted with dark grout if that is available (trust us, it looks cleaner for far longer). Heavy glasses that won't smash as easily as delicate Champagne flutes. Hefty mugs, plates and bowls, preferably from IKEA or a range that can be repurchased if the dinner set diminishes over time. Plug sockets that are screwed into the wall as securely as an ATM cash machine.

Damage is a sticky area for guests and owners alike. Charging guests when there is any doubt about broken or missing items is plain wrong. It won't win you repeat guests or positive reviews. Just the opposite. Most people are fundamentally decent and do not set out to purposely break things during their holiday or short stay. They would rather be sitting on a beach or perusing a museum instead.

Usage instructions that are to the point and clear are a good way to mitigate damage. A laminated set of easy to understand guidelines for turning on the dishwasher, managing the boiler, switching from Netflix to DVD and everything else will limit the amount of buttons pressed in anger when electronic items "don't work".

Always, always, always print instructions for your guests, as well as for your Meet & Greet person or agency, detailing where to shut off your water, gas and electricity in case of emergency. Failure to do this can cause thousands in damages. We've seen the inability of a harried guest to locate a water stopcock at its watery worst.

3) Factoring in wear, tear, insurance and repair

Let's use restaurants as an example. Like hotels or apartment hosts, they have to factor in some damage and repair.

We've all seen the patron who goes white as his restaurant tablecloth bleeds red wine and the sound of broken glass alerts everyone to his embarrassing misdemeanour. The discreet waiter then appears from nowhere, still smiling, and cleans up with as little inconvenience as possible. The sommelier may provide another bottle, on the house, poured with another smile.

Few diners receive or even expect a bill for cleaning the tablecloth or for payment of the smashed glass when they leave the restaurant. It's simply an ongoing and expected cost of doing business in that particular industry.

Short term letting follows the same rules. As a rough rule of thumb you should expect to put back into your rental property between 5% and 10% of your earnings to cover wear and tear – more likely the latter figure. In Pebbles' experience of managing fairly upmarket properties, around

80% of owners have put back about 10% per year over a five-year period.

Owners are always advised to acquire a good landlord's insurance policy that covers renting your home, or a part of it. You wouldn't let someone drive your car without insurance because you know accidents happen. So of course you'd use the same philosophy on your prize asset: your home. A solid policy will also litigate against the unlikely event that anything goes seriously wrong.

Some policies offer great cover. Often you can claim for all manner of lost bookings and damage. None of the insurance policies are particularly expensive. Probably because the bean counters know what we are telling you here: damage doesn't happen very often in your home, nor does it often happen when guests stay.

If it needs saying again, any host of any space should not be overly concerned about damage. By way of example, Pebbles take around 3,500 bookings a year and have less than 100 cases of damage a year (excluding things like broken wine glasses and missing teaspoons). That is less than a 3% ratio.

Most guests are respectful but accidents can happen or an inconsiderate guest may occasionally book. When it happens to you, it's obviously upsetting. But if the damage is small, you should see it as part of the cost of your business and accept that it occurs for the level of return you are achieving. If the damage is large it should always be recoverable from your insurance.

Still unhappy? Add up how much income you've made this year then subtract how much you've forked out in breakages. This should prove how these little setbacks are part and parcel of running a lucrative business.

4) The five-year lifecycle of your property

It is important with any investment to be open to further outlay as market influences dictate. In these exciting times in the rental space sector we advise all owners to take stock every year and plan ahead. Pebbles have noticed a general timeline trend in the 180 apartments they have under management, which we're certain dovetails with most rental properties.

Year one is an exciting time. You are slowly learning what your typical clients want. You're also learning what they tend to break. For example, regular guests at a beach hut in Brazil's Bahia province might dirty the towels beyond repair, while guests at a studio in Icelandic capital Reykjavik might be adept at trekking snow-strewn boots across the parquet floor. You therefore source a cheap supply of towels (in Brazil) or offer free indoor slippers for your guests to use (in Iceland).

Years two and three are even better. By printing off your booking calendar for the previous year, and taking into account local wedding seasons and prime business times, you can better plan and raise prices during peak times. If you're renting a spare room you might even choose to vacate your own home and rent the entire space for your peak month. You'd be surprised how many people do. During these golden years there are normally few ongoing costs aside from breakages and minor wear and tear. If you're doing things right, this is when your happy guests tell others about your space and how lovely you are to work with.

Year four is also good. Your regular customers keep booking. Favourite customers are emailed six months in advance and treated to flowers and croissants on arrival. Wear and tear is more advanced however. Technology has also moved on so that the iPod and TV you installed way back when might have to be replaced.

That's why year five seems to be the cut off point in the short term letting game. It's unlikely that you'll enjoy the same level of rental income as years two and three if you've been renting the space for five years or more. Neither do hotels. There's a natural cycle as the hotel moves from the new-kid-on the-block to "looking a bit tired" on its TripAdvisor reviews.

As much as it hurts, you can't keep giving your place a minor facelift in order to keep bookings regular. Neither can a hotel. You have to accept that shiny, bigger, hipper and brighter properties will come and invade your space. You will have to move down to second-tier for a while until you are ready to start the cycle again.

The good news is, after you renovate your property after five or so years, you shouldn't have to market it as hard. You will enjoy a successful flow of repeat bookings and word of mouth, and you can justify price increases to your customer base that has been loyally built up and honed over the years. You'll also be the new kid on the block again, with all the attractions that go with it.

Conversely, the truly new kids on the block have it all to do. Don't think for a minute they are gaining a better return than you are. They won't be as they're not established yet. They have a lot to learn. (Unless of course they've bought this book. Sorry about that.)

Our tip is to avoid doing little by little to smarten up your property. Unless there is an obvious part of the guest offering which is letting the place down, changing one bit but leaving the rest as usual won't have much of an impact. For example, if you just install a new sofa, you have to change the photo of that sofa. If nothing else has changed that's is a fair bit of work for little overall gain. Your photos may even look worse with your new sofa at the centre surrounded by grubby older items. What's the point in investing then having little extra to shout about?

5) Renovating your rental space

After five long years of wear and tear (or six or seven at a stretch) you'll net more cash if you redecorate your space. When you bite the renovation bullet it's best to baton down the hatches, plan and prepare. We can't stress that loud enough: meticulously plan then methodically prepare. Take stock on what is working for other property owners. Look at pricing across any competitors. Look to see what's changed in your area. Perhaps you've been lucky enough to have a business complex built nearby. Perhaps there's a children's theme park being built. Upgrading your efforts from five years ago is what you should do this time, in a more guest-accentuated manner.

That said, the world moves quickly and your space needs to move with it. If there's a conference centre being constructed next year, perhaps your planning stage should take longer and you should divide that large two bedroom apartment into two studios for sole business travellers. If a sporting venue is being built, perhaps the way to go is a budget space with bunk beds, bike storage, keycode access for late trainers and a shared breakfast space.

Once you have a plan, let your regulars know it. Even the largest hotels email guests to say: "We're sorry the Wi-Fi was slow (or beds were soft, or restaurant was closed) during your stay, we're now upgrading and would love you to try it out first".

There's no harm in contacting your guests at the end of their stay to tell them: "We hope you enjoyed staying with us this summer. We also thought we'd share our exciting plans with you. If you visit us again in 2018 you'll find a new hot tub/teppanyaki grill/surfboard storage room. If you have any feedback for us before we start the improvements, please let us know". Then call in the decorators/builders/fengshui experts and relaunch your cavehome/caravan/apartment with a bang.

Be careful on your overhaul. There's a reason hotels bring in interior designers. These experts know what will look hot next season and they also know what items will last the long haul. Don't be swayed by end of range tiles or bargain fixtures to save money. This will almost certainly be a false economy.

One of the biggest mistakes we have seen is a bathroom refit where the owner went for cut-price sinks and a nasty plastic shower cubicle. "I want to raise my rental price to reflect my new bathroom," he told us. We replied: "Great that you've spent €4,000 on the bathroom but we don't think anyone will pay more for your apartment based on those low-cost white tiles. Putting the price up will only make you more expensive than your competitors"

Our advice, which was taken with tears, was based upon how the bathroom looked on the new image. Photos really do tell a thousand words. From the image we uploaded online, no potential guest could tell if the bathroom dated from the 1990s or from the 21st century. If he'd spent just €250 more on tiles from a modern range his property would have looked fresher and newer – and he could have raised his rental price accordingly.

Put simply, when you make improvements guests need to see how things have been improved. Nowhere is this truer than when choosing kitchens and bathrooms, especially when it comes to tiling.

Boring? Certainly. Good-to-know? You bet.

Remember that when your upgrade is done, you need to re-shoot high-quality photos then spend time uploading them to your advertising space. Descriptions also need an overhaul, get a friend to proof read and suggest changes to your marketing spiel. All this takes time. And if you're bringing in a professional photographer, copywriter or other professional, money. Bear the costs of time and effort in mind during your planning. You get more for your buck doing a big job than a piecemeal one.

Chapter 12 written in stone

1) Recognise that you will probably have to put between 5% and 10% of your annual rental income back into the property. Or walk away from this project now.

2) It's expensive and time-consuming. But planning for emergencies and investing in fittings that won't go wrong will save you much more money in the long run.

3) Wear and tear setbacks are part and parcel of running a lucrative business. Large-scale damage very rarely happens, but a landlord's insurance policy will guard against the costs involved.

4) After printing easy money for four years or so, be prepared to peel off a few notes to make yourself the new kid on the block once again.

5) Plan carefully and upgrade prudently. Better to wait until you can afford the right upgrade than to do half a job.

Chapter 13: I fought the law and the law won

"Other governments are waiting to witness the tourism versus residents outcome of this opening skirmish."

"Laws are like cobwebs, which may catch small flies, but let wasps and hornets break through."

Jonathan Swift

Barcelona City Hall possesses a singular document. It sets out the world's first tourism accommodation management plan. The PDF claims that: "an uncontrolled increase in tourist accommodation is putting neighbourhoods at risk".

The local government's plan is to: "conserve people's right to housing, rest and privacy, sustainable mobility and a healthy environment". It's a noble goal. And one that takes direct aim at Barcelona's short term rental market which, they argue, has caused over-gentrification to occur. "There are neighbourhoods where the floating population is greater than the residential population," says the document, "like the Gótico area where the ratio is 61.5%".

In November 2016, Barcelona's left-wing mayor Ada Colau said it was: "unacceptable that there are thousands of apartments operating illegally without a permit, not paying taxes and causing a nuisance to neighbours". That year Airbnb and HomeAway were fined €600,000 each. Local residents are encouraged to call in illegal renters using a webpage in Spanish, Catalan, English, French or German. It's an outright attack on the short term rental scene.

It's also a clouded picture. The average Airbnb host in Barcelona earns just €5,000 a year in rental revenue. The Catalan capital remains the only city in the world to fine the web rental portal, which brings around 300,000 free-spending groups to the city each year. The firm responded to the mayor's tirade by stating that: "Airbnb is part of the solution in Barcelona and it is disappointing to see City Hall intimidate locals with archaic rules that threaten an economic lifeline for thousands. There is a contradiction at the heart of tourism policies in Barcelona, which favour commercial operators (like hotels). Home sharing puts money in the pockets of locals."

So who's right? It's difficult to assess the benefits of increased tourism and host income to an area vis-a-vis the alleged costs to local society. Especially as, despite extensive email exchanges, the three planning departments questioned by this book (Barcelona, London and Berlin) declined to answer specific queries or to be interviewed.

Alas, it may not matter who's right. Our research shows that it's who drafts the law that calls the shots.

In Berlin, Germany, a similar law has been implemented. It's called the Law on the Prohibition of Misuse of Housing, which with Teutonic linguistic efficiency has become the *Zweckentfremdungsverbot*. Catchy, huh?

Less prosaically, it's an effective ban on Airbnb, Wimdu and other short term letting websites. The mathematics behind the law tells the story. Over the past five years, studio apartments that once rented in the edgy Neukölln area for €500 per month now book out for €75 per night.

Half a million Berlin visitors stayed in Airbnb apartments in the city in 2015 alone, no doubt greatly adding to the local economy. A study commissioned by Airbnb showed that nearly half of hosts earn below Berlin's median household income over €1,650 per month. And that Airbnb guests spent more time and money in the city than traditional hotel guests, albeit – city officials claim – at an alleged cost to local society.

To this end, unregistered rental apartments can be fined €100,000 by Berlin authorities. Hosts renting part of their space, or making an unpaid home exchange, are exempted from the law.

The above examples from Barcelona and Berlin cite the world's toughest 'anti-Airbnb' laws. Most local governments plan to work hand-in-hand with rental websites to boost city tourism through tricky economic times, especially when local occupancy tax and rental tax is collected by rental websites at the same time. But other governments are waiting to witness the tourism versus residents outcome of this opening skirmish.

Such unpredictability is a salutary lesson to anyone embarking on their short term rental journey. The next chapter points out what changes could occur in the industry next.

Chapter 14: Fifty shades of legal grey

"If arbitration will take an entire morning, is pursuing a $150 breakage fee the best use of your time?"

> "The large print giveth and the small print taketh away."
> **Tom Waits**

This holiday letting Klondike, this Airbnb Gold Rush, is in legal disarray. Governments, local councils and travel insurers haven't caught up with the short term rental boom.

Not that any global legal rulings will happen soon. It will take years for these institutions to decide how to tax, govern or legislate the sharing economy, which remains one of the most rapid and significant economic upheaval of all time.

It will take even longer for insurers to take stock of this boom. Just imagine this legal conundrum for one moment: Who should pay up for an accident caused by a Portuguese cleaner inside a Spanish villa owned by a Swiss national that was booked using an American credit card by a Mexican citizen on a holiday rental website based in Luxembourg?

That scenario is well within the realms of possibility. In fact, it has probably occurred several times.

Furthermore, in the unlikely event that the proverbial hits the fan, don't expect much legal help. Airbnb is simply a peer-to-peer advertising platform that takes a fee for connecting you to a paying guest. It is not keen to involve itself in cross-border disputes concerning anything from a broken plate to a broken leg. Visa is more interested in taking a cut on credit card transactions than pursuing legal redress against a booking made many moons ago.

In all cases it's best to be aware of the rules. And to protect yourself as much as humanly possible. You'd be amazed how stupid guests –and hosts – can be. And as you'll read later in the chapter, we've witnessed more than our fair share of both.

We hope our experience may help you. That said, there are over 190 legal jurisdictions on the planet and we are not about to delve into the complexities of each one. The following paragraphs should serve as a rough guide, not as legal gospel. If you want legal advice don't buy a book, pay a lawyer instead.

1) What happens when you can't fully honour a booking

If you're nice – and we're sure you are - this is one of the scariest parts of being a host. That shrinking feeling when you realise you have to let down your guest when they have entrusted you with their trip. Perhaps the shower fitting in your ski chalet springs a leak on December 31st – just as your guests are due to fly in, leaving them with only one bathroom to service eight tired guests. Horrors of horrors, perhaps you have double booked your apartment by accident.

The latter should never happen. If you are only advertising in one place or have a rental agent it probably won't. Yet if you are marketing the rental space yourself and are advertising on multiple booking websites, you must, must, must keep a firm diary on your computer desktop or on paper, detailing which guest has booked when and what date they are departing. Have a partner or friend check your workings twice over. It's that important.

Incidents inside apartments do happen, especially in older buildings. When disaster strikes it's best to thoroughly explain the issue to your guest as soon as possible. They will be upset, but most will understand once it is explained to them properly and especially when you offer them an alternative.

If your clients can't stay in the apartment they booked, guests often prefer to believe that you have double booked or accepted a better offer. It's human nature to feel aggrieved if your holiday plans are scuppered. Showing them the issue first hand: be it a collapsed ceiling, dangerous leak or expensive plumbing quote will give them a stake in the problem and let them understand what issues you are working with. Email them, or better still call them, at the earliest opportunity.

Moving guests who are obviously disappointed involves a lot of work. Therefore, try not uproot guests whenever possible but instead persuade them to stay and accept the property with a discount. While not always possible, having guests stay put is always far less stressful and often cheaper than moving them. Make it worth their while as guests are entitled to a full refund if they prefer not to stay in your partially damaged property. The added work involved in moving guests can be considerable, and sometimes guests also expect to be compensated for the inconvenience.

If you don't have the luxury of your management agent moving guests for you, build up a network of pals. When leaks and other catastrophes strike, it's good to have friends who can help out your guests on the rare occasions when problems occur. Build up this network. As well as these fellow hosts helping you this time, you'll be offered some last-minute bookings from them too.

2) When to suck it up

If you are taking damage deposits by credit card via a booking website like VRBO, or are working with a third party agency who manages your property, know this: If you are planning to charge a guest for damage you will have to prove beyond any doubt that they caused the mutilation of your carpet/sofa/iPad/bathroom/sheets.

The first step is to rule out three things. Number one is wear and tear, which causes rips and cracks over time, especially in stingily managed properties. Number two is technical fault outside a guest's control, which can magically disable routers and stop dishwashers from working. Number three is guests mistreating an item that they're unfamiliar with, just as you bash the buttons of a recalcitrant TV control or air-conditioning unit while in a hotel room.

As most breakages, leakages and damages fall into the three categories we just mentioned, you might have to et it pass.

If there is room for uncertainty then whoever is the judge – be it the credit card company brought in to arbitrate, Airbnb or your letting agency – they will have to rule in the guest's favour where there is a smidgen of doubt. If you bear this in mind from the beginning, you can avoid a lot of work, saving both parties much heartache and avoid negative reviews.

Even if your guest is obviously guilty of causing, for example, $150 of damage, weigh up the situation. If the arbitration involved takes up an entire morning, ask yourself this: is pursuing a charge against them the best use of your time?

The conclusion? With minor damages it's best to suck it up. Take it on the chin. Bear in mind that charging a guest $25 for two broken glasses may well garner a negative review. But thanking that guest by email and urging them to revisit might garner a repeat booking, with all the extra income that it will bring.

In short, renting your spare room, holiday home or luxury apartment will cost you at least something in on-going damages. But this is a relatively small price to pay for the annual income it will provide.

3) When to pursue legal action against a guest

Now we're moving into serious territory. And it's potentially more painful than childbirth, with the six months of sleepless nights and gross expense that follows. One of the authors of this book is a qualified lawyer with six years of post-training practice in litigation. Take it from us: pursuing legal action is costly, time-consuming and, on occasion, more trouble than its worth.

The tricky situation in the short term letting boom concerns jurisdiction. For example, if you rent a property in your home county on a long term let, and your tenant does not pay, you can sue them. Best of all you are likely to win if you go through normal legal channels in your home country, where both of you reside.

However, the chances are that your short term letting guest will not come from your home country. Prosecuting a client from Bolivia or Bhutan will be far more problematic if you are a Swedish national with a holiday home in Bali. Even if you successfully sue the Canadian who trashed your Caribbean hideaway (an extremely rare occurrence as we explain in Chapter 8), arranging a bailiff and court order to force payment might be more excruciating than a night out in Winnipeg, Manitoba.

Fortunately, non-payment is rare. In our experience over 99% of bookings operate without issue. Fake credit cards or dodgy details are filtered by sophisticated software which involves three party checks of the booking website, the acquiring bank and the card issuer.

4) The legalities of working with a big rental website

If you have a space to rent in a crowded market, you'll need to join forces with a company with strong advertisng credentials to get your space seen.

That's old news. But you'll have to agree to their terms and fall in line with their practices, often giving up your own preferred way of doing things. The well-crafted conditions will have been drafted by legal experts to protect the person paying for them, not you. The terms will likely cover every scenario in their favour. The bigger the company, the more likely they won't care so much if you join in or not, and so their terms can be very stringent. They are not up for negotiation.

Take Booking.com for example. Their Accommodation Agreement from 2016 states that commission payments under point 2.4 are due without deduction and:
Booking.com is not responsible for the correctness and completeness of the information (including credit card details) and dates provided by Guests and Booking.com is not responsible for the payment obligations of the Guests relating to their (online) reservation.

That's a lot of legal blah-blah. Both rental agencies and hoteliers believe this to mean that should a guest book your property through Booking.com and choose a pay on arrival option and not turn up, or after they've left you find out the card used was fraudulent, not only will you not get paid for the booking, but you still are liable to Booking.com for their hefty commission. Harsh. Just remember that the company is out to protect its booking fee, not your yearly income.

Many sites, including TripAdvisor's HolidayLettings, will allow you limited contact with your guest until after they have paid their deposit. Calling a potential guest for an old-fashioned chat is no longer an option on these sites. Of course, this is so that host and guest don't make a private deal and cut TripAdvisor out of its commission. In practice it means that the guest and host can only correspond through a TripAdvisor email box, so there is unfortunately room for misunderstandings.

The above is now the cost of partnering with big booking portals – and their global advertising reach. The way to move forward is to type as much as humanly possible in the text of your listing, including any frequently asked questions. You can refer potential guests to this page. Take heart, give a good service, and they'll book directly with you next time.

Using a big web portal to take bookings? You will also see that many offer the option for the host to insure their space against damage. We're afraid that many policies are just marketing ploys with little substance. If you read the small print, many host protection policies only come into play when you can prove your own homeowner insurance is exhausted, and your guests' insurance is also exhausted. How much time and effort is that going to take is certainly worth considering.

So what is not covered by a guests' insurance, and then your own insurance, that then is going to be worth claiming for? Only you can decide after reading what your home insurance covers. Always pay attention to the small print before signing up. If it's important to you, have it reviewed by a legal friend.

Getting an insurance policy looked over is easier than you think. Simply Google the host policy insurance you are thinking about purchasing and read on. Many insurance experts give opinions on the most common policies online. Take their advice on board then make up your own mind. Buying this book may have saved you a bundle already.

Finally, if you're taking bookings through any booking portal there are safe ways to avoid legal action for damage inside your apartment. Request a worldwide accepted credit card as deposit and authorize a payment for potential damage through a merchant bank. Or add a large damage waiver on Airbnb or similar rental website which can likewise be returned on the safe departure of your guests. Or opt for a Paypal deposit you will give back at the end of the booking.

Now the good news. Whatever you decide, never lose sight that 99 transactions out of 100 will work just fine. Ok, you might get your bad one in the first year of renting, but at least then it's probably out of the way. All the majority of guests want to do is enjoy a nice holiday or business trip in your Auckland apartment or Tampa treehouse.

5) The People vs Airbnb

Airbnb and other short term bookings websites have changed lives and made possible a totally different sort of holiday experience. But such websites have been buffeted by legal challenges from across the globe.

In November 2016, Germany's Minister of Economic Affairs called for stronger regulation of booking platforms and portals such as Airbnb, maintaining that many "sharing economy" firms were only successful because they ignored the insurance and liability issues. He also claimed that hosts using booking platforms did not always pay their taxes properly. In the face of housing shortages Berlin authorities pressed the nuclear button in mid-2016: the city has effectively banned residents from renting entire apartments out on Airbnb. It's still legal to rent out a spare room, as long as the space takes up no more than 50% of the total area.

According to figures quoted on global tourism channel Tourism Review, Buenos Aires has an alleged 16,000 'informal temporary rentals' that rarely pay VAT, income taxes or social security contributions, which competing hotels and licensed rental agencies are obliged to pay. However, authority plans to register these properties, and therefore earn taxes from spaces that tourists actively seek out, have been lazier than an Argentine waiter during a World Cup final.

In Paris the fine-grinding French bureaucracy is doing something about it. Through summer 2016 Airbnb notched a 20% increase for bookings in the French capital. That may be a huge bonus for local tourism, but Parisian hotels, many of which are notoriously lazy in their quest to capture a clued-up travelling public, have become jealous. In many French cities Airbnb must now collect a tourism tax on behalf of its clients, just as hotels and rental agencies have done for decades, while hosts themselves must register their property with the local council and pay taxes on income gained.

In 2017 Airbnb's system started automatically limiting Greater London's 'entire home' listings to just 90 days a year. This was in response to the announcement that the British capital was going to enforce long-standing rules that limit rentals to a quarter of the year.

Don't be surprised if such laws come to your city soon. Any new owner who embarks on this potentially lucrative project needs to be aware that booking platforms, legal rules and taxation costs could look very different three years on. Check local legislation but don't let it put you off. Any company that has poured tens of millions guests into the global tourism economy in a mere few years is acclaimed, vilified and scapegoated (depending on your opinion) in equal measure.

6) How to steer away from legal disaster and distress

The short term letting boom that has led tourists to book vintage rail carriages in Australia – and your Aunt Anne to rent out the stable at the bottom of her garden – has left millions of properties in a legal grey area. There are two million owners and counting on Airbnb alone. If a guest slips and breaks a leg on your shared stairwell, who's fault is it? Moreover, who will pay the hospital bill?

The list of possibilities is as endless as the disasters are potentially unlikely. But if a host provides a free meal on arrival and accidentally hospitalises the guest with food poisoning, you can bet your bottom dollar, euro or pound that the guest's travel insurance won't want to know about it... but someone will still have to cough up in terms of lost holiday and missed flights.

Covering yourself against legal redress is a two-fold affair. The rules may differ in the 193 countries that make up the United Nations. So these four achingly boring points we're about to make should serve as a guide only.

Firstly, cover your backside. Every vehicle lot tells drivers they park their car at their own risk. McDonalds reminds all customers that the coffee they are holding is hot. Most things are blindingly obvious. But that shouldn't stop you pointing it out to cover yourself.

Make sure you have a contract or at least a list of items (often called a customer charter) that you offer each guest for the price. Most times, if you are working with a web portal, your listing will act as your customer charter.

If you opt for a contract it doesn't have to be complicated. There are thousands of free ones you can use on the web. Beware of copyright. Enough said.

Your contract or terms also do not need to be adorned with pen and ink in our digital age. Over half the world now accepts electronic signatures as binding including the USA, New Zealand, Hong Kong and most of Europe. If you want to know where your country stands on it, type "Adobe Electronic Signatures" into Google and you'll soon have the info.

The key to a document being legally binding is just this: were the parties involved intending to be bound by the document and its terms? An email from the guest saying they have read and agreed is – in our non-binding opinion – all you'll likely need for renting out a space casually. Of course, this is just a guide and if you want to be 100% protected, you need to seek a lawyer's advice in your own jurisdiction.

Secondly, don't take unnecessary risks. We know property owners who take the most unfathomable risks for the tiniest of gains. For example, one lady in Nice offers an airport pick-up included in her Airbnb rental.

The guests find the service welcoming, straightforward and less expensive than hailing a cab. But if the host crashes and serious injury results, she's up the creek. Without a paddle.

If the lady's insurance firm discovers she has been offering a 'taxi' service she won't be covered. She may therefore be personally liable for all medical fees and compensation. In France, that is going to be expensive even for minor injuries; for severe injuries she's probably looking at debt until she dies. That we're all friends together in the new economy goes straight out of the window when lawyers are called in to seek hundreds of thousands in disability damages.

The possibilities we don't think about until disaster strikes are always the scariest. To avoid them, don't do them. That means don't offer airport pick-up unless you drive a taxi as your day job and they pay you a fare. Don't offer a babysitting service unless you're a fully qualified (and legally insured) Mary Poppins. Don't include bikes, skates or skiing equipment unless you've also provided some sort of waiver that to use them is at the guests' own risk. And if you must provide snacks on arrival buy them plastic wrapped from a supermarket. We know we sound like killjoys, but just don't.

Thirdly, and this is super boring, but make sure you have any legal permissions from your local council necessary to rent out your space. Google your own location if you're not sure. We've already mentioned how cities and local governments are reacting to the sharing economy. In San Francisco, USA, all would-be hosts must register in person with the San Francisco Planning Department before listing on a website. In London, United Kingdom, if you are letting for more than 90 days, you may now need planning permission.

Of course, most licenses and permissions are a cinch to obtain with a few clicks or phone calls. But if you don't have them your insurance may baulk at paying out.

Fourthly and finally, live by this golden rule. Imagine yourself in a witness box and ask yourself "did I do the right thing all those months ago". Laws differ in every country so this is an amateur guide only, but most courtrooms are about convincing a jury that your actions were mitigated by honesty, not by negligence or avarice. If, in good faith, you have provided working smoking alarms, suitable door locks and installed child safety bars around a swimming pool you will hopefully receive the benefit of the doubt.

Although disaster may never strike, if it does then at the very least you can convince a prosecutor that you did your best to do the right thing at the time.

7) When an Uber driver becomes an employee

We are living in increasingly bizarre digital financial system. It's increasingly unclear who employs who, which has a bearing on the short term rentals market.

Uber is a case in point. From its official launch in 2011, it has turned a century-old taxi industry completely on its head. In the process it has become a $50bn company operating in over 500 cities. The general public have fallen for the product. It's now also got litigation to deal with as more established enterprises fight back to protect their industry or at least make it a level playing field.

From Nice Airport, an official taxi to the city centre costs around €65. Official taxis have huge costs to cover including license fee and insurance. With Uber it's around €22. Recent demands for Uber to comply with some licensing regulations saw their prices rise. Most cities have a similar taxi-to-Uber price ratio.

Like many similar firms, many in the news, Uber has also ignited a powder keg of employee rights. Most drivers are affiliated with the company not as employees but as contractors, even if Uber is their principal source of revenue. In most countries those definitions split differently in terms of employment rights, taxation, overtime, holiday pay, minimum wage and so on, with both positives and negatives for the company, its competitors, its drivers and local governments.

How does that affect the short term rental of my beach shack in Goa, India? By making sure that the people who market, clean and meet your guests are not 'employed' by you.

Employment law and regulation differs widely country to country, state to state. There's no clear cut set of rules we can give you. But we can offer pointers: If you task your cleaner to arrive at a certain time each week for a certain amount of hours on a long term arrangement, some jurisdictions will regard this as employment, with all its legal requirements that go with it. In all cases check your cleaner is registered as self-employed or assure them in writing (on paper or digitally) that you're asking them to provide an ad hoc service, that they can refuse to work at any time. If in doubt use a professional cleaning agency instead.

Chapter 14 written in stone

1) If you mix up your booking dates, expect no sympathy. And have a Plan B and Plan C in case things go wrong, including a plumber on speed dial and a friend across the hall.

2) As many breakages, leakages and damages are caused by wear and tear, technical fault or item mistreatment, you might have to factor a small amount of damage into your profit margin.

3) Legal action is best avoided by charging a refundable damage waiver than you return to guests after departure. As pursuing a recalcitrant guest through the courts is time-consuming and excruciatingly expensive, it's best avoided.

4) A big rental apartment booking website probably won't cover you in a worse case scenario. Guests do silly thinks on holiday, frequently while drunk, so insure against their most outlandish scenarios.

5) Airbnb and its competitors are here to stay. But progressive legal challenges will probably force their users to pay more taxes and abide by local rules as the years go on.

6) Read the small print in your letting insurance. Don't pick up guests from the airport. And try not to poison them.

7) Do you 'employ' your Meet & Great lady or your cleaning guy, or just contract them on an ad hoc basis? Get this right or you could blow your annual return.

Chapter 15: Maximising revenue becomes automated

"In 2018 over 20% of accommodation bookings worldwide will be for short term rentals. But tens of millions of hosts are missing out by charging the same flat rates over the entire year."

> "Anticipate the difficult by managing the easy."
>
> **Lao Tzu**

Ian McHenry started his career as an airline revenue manager. These are the guys who, two decades ago, created basic algorithms to allow companies like Europe's easyJet and America's Southwest Airlines to charge more or less based upon demand on a particular date.

Airline revenue management is now commonplace. If you book an advance flight to Venice, Italy for a rainy February vacation the price will be keen. Conversely, if you book a last-minute trip to Venice in mid-August, where demand is high and seats are scarce, the algorithm will spit out a take-it-or-leave-it price from hell. As in enough to make you choke on your €22 bellini cocktail in Harry's Bar.

A decade later the computer algorithms were far more advanced. Airlines had taken the bait but hotels still charged the same rack rates for months on end. No extra fee was added to wedding seasons, weekends or conference periods. Again McHenry helped change all that, allowing hotels to squeeze far more revenue out of a Saturday night skier in Whistler, Canada, or an Oktoberfest beer drinker in Munich, Germany. Prices became automatically linked to supply and demand.

"That's why I was shocked that no revenue maximization system existed for rental websites," says McHenry. "In 2018 over 20% of accommodation bookings worldwide will be for short term rentals. But tens of millions of hosts are missing out by charging the same flat rates over the entire year." Airbnb offers similar price management tips but these are rigid and ineffective, claims McHenry, mostly because their system tries to increase bookings and therefore reservation commissions, rather than increase the amount that hosts charge.

That's why he created Beyond Pricing in 2013. The tool can log-in to your Airbnb or HomeAway account (the site that governs VRBO, FeWo-Direkt, Arbitel and all the rest) and automatically update your prices to boost revenue. Like all algorithms, Beyond Pricing is cleverer than you are. Simply put, it uses far more data than you have access to and can update prices on a minute-by-minute basis. It takes into account seasonality, weekends and spikes in demand far in advance, based on weather data, hotel stats and sudden increases in rental demand.

"By way of example Uber doesn't know that it's raining," says McHenry. "Beyond Pricing might not know that a rock concert has just been announced in your town. Instead the big data out there is automatically distilled onto your price page to boost your rates on a certain day, weekend or week to take account of new information." Most users claim a year-on-year increase in revenue of between 10% and 40%. Beyond Pricing charges a fee of 1% of your rental revenue for this service.

McHenry cites the example of the eclipse in Oregon, USA in August 2017. His clients didn't know about the reported solar occurrence – Beyond Pricing's computer certainly didn't – but the tools that kicked in after a TV show highlighted the event boosted hosts' prices six-fold. They sold out fast. And apartment owners that charged a regular rack rate? They sold out instantly too. At base price. Sad.

The company's success rode on the coat tails of the big rental portals. In early 2014 the firm was managing $4m of bookings per month. By early 2017 they were managing $4m of reservations *per week*. Of course, hosts can still override, lower or raise their prices with just one click across their entire rental presence if they disagree with Beyond Pricing's costing tips. The project has proved so successful that vacation rental giants like onefinestay and

Iambnb use the service for the thousands of properties that they manage.

Beyond Pricing is part of a wider trend. Not just an automated revenue management tool that gives little guys the tools that big hotel chains use (others include Pricelabs and Everbooked). But also in third party add-ons like Guesty, which manages guest liaison via Booking.com, VRBO and everything else, and Lockitron, an electronic door lock that can be unlocked via an App from thousands of miles away, taking away the need for face-to-face key swaps. "Short term rentals are a $100bn a year market so there are hundreds of add-ons and plug-ins to make managing your space easier," concludes McHenry. "If 50% of hosts aren't using at least one of them in 2018 I'll buy you a goddam bellini in Venice."

The future isn't just bright. It's automated.

Chapter 16: Onwards and upwards

"Making money while sitting on the beach. It really happens you know."

> "Only put off until tomorrow what you are willing to die having left undone."
>
> **Pablo Picasso**

The party has started. Guests from every nation, currencies in every domination, lay latent and untapped.

It's now time to join in. Although we advise spending longer on the task, you can get a listing for your rental asset online in under 60 minutes. The whole world can then see it. Quite possibly one of those hundreds of millions of people who take a vacation or a business trip each year will book it. All they need is a credit card and they're good to go.

But you have to get on it. As Woody Allen once said: "Eighty percent of success is showing up." You can't win without taking part.

Fortunately, making money while you sleep has never been easier. Two decades ago you could only advertise your guest space via word-of-mouth or though a magazine or supermarket advertisement. The marketing reach was, at most, thousands.

A decade ago the Internet offered a client reach of millions but the tools, the websites and the ease of contacting potential punters across the planet weren't there. Back then the web wasn't for everyone.

Now the Internet is for your silver surfing mother, your eight-year-old nephew, your great aunt Joan. The world wide web is made for ease and speed. Anyone can connect with the near two billion users of Facebook, around 30% of the entire world, in just a few clicks. Who would have thought that would ever be possible?

As we saw in the last chapter, websites like Beyond Pricing make the task of renting your place even easier too. You don't even have to 'think' about setting prices. There's an app to do it for you, just as there is a simple online tool for everything.

In the forthcoming era of the driverless car there will be no excuse for not riding across the country tomorrow.

There is currently no excuse for not making money from the property you pay so much to upkeep.

If you are new to this lucrative game then this final chapter is a summation of our book's ethos. We wish you luck. If you've have already joined the short term rental revolution and are using our guide to squeeze even more from your asset, read on. We'll reveal how to make even more money in 2018, 2019 and beyond.

1) A history lesson: after the Big Bang

The market for vacation, business and other short let accommodation has quite literally exploded. It took nearly a century from the invention of the car in 1886 for the motor vehicle to become a commonly owned item worldwide.

Airbnb has been around for less than 10 years and is already a household name.

The automobile industry has consolidated over 100 years. Decades ago there were thousands of car brands across the world. Now that Renault owns Nissan, and Volkswagen owns Audi, Porsche and Škoda, and so on and so forth, just seven automotive companies produce the majority of the world's cars.

The short term rental industry is also consolidating, albeit at its habitual breakneck pace. Guests want to book accommodation as quickly and easily as possible. They demand the greatest selection with as few clicks as possible. Increasingly, there is less room for minnows.

By 2018, there will be more 'consolidator' booking sites. One burgeoning example is Tripping, which allows guests to search through eight million properties across Booking.com, Roomorama, Stopsleepgo and VRBO courtesy of one website. (Airbnb has *only* two million properties.)

As long as you list with one of these sites it shouldn't matter. And if those portals operate as a dodgy corporate monopoly in decades to come, another usurper will smash them with better, cheaper, more personable service. Remember dominant players like Microsoft, IBM and British Airways? These firms are now dwarfed by Apple, Samsung and Ryanair.

What makes a greater difference to the consumer are tie-ups between the largest companies. In 2016 Southwest Airlines, America's largest domestic carrier, partnered with Booking.com, which reserves hotels as well as vacation rental homes. If your property was listed on the latter site, it could be booked by a customer on the Southwest website with the final check-in managed by yourself. Expect other rental portals to tie-in with airlines, rail firms and travel agents soon. This means more reservations all round. Staying in a rental apartment or spare room will become just as 'normal' as staying in a hotel.

As the market matures we predict a flight to quality. When easyJet, Europe's second largest airline, launched in 1995 it was cheap and cheerful. Now it's known as a business carrier. Two thirds of its passengers earn over €40,000 ($43,000) a year.

In 2015 Airbnb launched its Business Travel Ready concept, where commerce-friendly apartments can be filtered by business travellers. Most are far nicer than hotels, not to mention cheaper. You would like to stay in one, and your boss would prefer you did too. We're in a market that is set to stay.

2) Travis's Law, and why Uber won't go away

Brad Stone is a Silicon Valley journalist. His stories for Bloomberg (*Uber and the Invasion of the Taxi Snatchers*) and books (*Amazon, the Everything Store*) render him the digital go-to.

His 2017 title, *The Upstarts: How Uber, Airbnb and the New Silicon Valley are Changing the World*, is the most telling. Like us, Stone quotes timely figures, such as how Uber is worth more than General Motors. What's interesting is a theory he introduces called 'Travis's Law'.

Travis Kalanick is the CEO of Uber. The firm's wildfire expansion led to regulatory issues, most which have been overridden by enlisting Uber users for help. Travis's Law states that politicians can be forced to accept a service better than the existing alternative by peer pressure alone.

London, United Kingdom offers the best example of Travis's Law. In June 2014 12,000 Black Cab taxi drivers brought the British capital to a standstill in an anti-Uber strike. Former Mayor, Boris Johnson, tried to legislate against the ride-hailing firm but was met with a petition from 200,000 Uber supporters roused using social media. All Johnson could say was: "we can't dis-invent the Internet". Uber and the technology behind it are here to stay. Incidentally, uptake of Uber app during the London taxi driver strike increased by 850%.

The short term rental market faces similar concerns. Many hotels have been resting on their laurels for years. They can offer desultory service and clueless reception staff because they're the only gig in town. The accommodation lobby is so strong that some cities have dissuaded councils from opening new hotels, so incumbents can sit back and watch their room prices rise. No more. To quote from singer-songwriter Paul Weller: 'The public gets what the public wants'. Especially if it has 720,000 Twitter followers, as Uber does.

Despite their youthfulness, the likes of Airbnb and HomeAway are now part of the furniture. Travis's Law means that any attempts to stop them from operating will draw ire from the millions of people that enjoy a second income from them. Plus the tens of millions of travellers who use the service.

Speaking of furniture, these web rental portals are like a Billy bookcase from Ikea: just too useful to throw away. (Note that 50 million Billys have been sold since 1979. And counting.)

3) It's not all about the money

Joining the short term rental revolution isn't just about being richer. It's about being free.

It's about the difference that the extra $400 a month or €10,000 a year – or more or less as your circumstance permits – will offer you.

The freedom to pay those bills that once scared you at 8am on a Tuesday morning. The freedom to retire earlier with a larger yearly income to spend on toys that your grandchildren will break within five minutes. The freedom to spend more on your next holiday (as you perform that mythical trick of making money while sitting on the beach). The freedom to retire to your holiday home when the mortgage has been paid off by rental guests.

There is a freedom that derives from having an extra leg to stand on. Let's look at the negative side first. If you lost your job a decade ago it meant the worst. Now that news is slightly less bad as you can rent out part or all of your home to help make ends meet.

And the positive side? If you keep your job *and* make a far greater annual income from your rental space, you can wear a better suit than your boss. Then sit next to him or her in meetings. Then Instagram photos of the two of you together, with you looking far, far better dressed. It's the small things isn't it?

There's also a freedom in uncluttering your home. Remember the retired couple in Chapter 2 who spent $108,000 on two storage units? The ones that kept a Fisher-Price children's cassette player in a rented box for 30 years? That could have been you. That's it, kiss that crap goodbye.

Freedom also comes from being your own boss. The money you make after reading this book will filter into your bank account the day after your first guests check-in. It's yours to keep. Don't spend it wisely. There's time for that later. Throw a party. Or buy a new pair of shoes. Buy two pairs.

There's also the friendships and the networking. A self-employed cartoonist or photographer who deposit their artworks around their space might open doors to future work. Like-minded guests who inhabit your spare room might find a space at your dinner table. It's been known to happen.

This venture could even be the first business you've ever started. In which case we hope it leads to greater things. A second home perhaps. Or an enterprise inspired when you realise how easy it is to market your product to several billion people at a time. Or how online payments have become so easy to manage that you can start an online business without having a garage full of stock.

Whatever this new opportunity means for you, we're rooting for you. Truly. Let us know how you get on.

4) That thing about the beach again...

Making money while sitting on the beach. Can we talk about it one more time please?

It really happens you know. Getting richer as you soak up the sun. Rental businesses small and large are run via apps. The mobile phones that belong to the authors of this book aren't the greatest (our children will only overload them with games) but our commerce is conducted from afar, our conversations with clients performed instantly from halfway across the world. Occasionally while sitting on the beach. More often while sitting on the toilet, but the idea of not wasting time at a desk is still there.

We've done the hard work set out in Chapter 4. (Remember when we told you to buy all those knives and forks and bedside lights? Boring.) Now we can sit back and let our guests pay us like we own a Hilton hotel.

There's room on the beach for you too. Members of this short term rental economy have also made money in the air, during a dancing contest and halfway through a cooking course. You don't have to sit on the toilet if you don't want to.

Many years ago one of the authors of this book learnt that they could rent out their entire home for $250 per night while they slept in a five-star hotel in Agadir, Morocco for $50 per night. That means waking up every day $200 richer – and that's before settling down for a day's work in the hotel's business centre. It's a trip that the author repeats for a month each year. It makes the author another $6,000 during that oh so special of months. Please note that the hotel offers all-you-can-consume meals and drinks in with the package. We highly recommend it.

You can make money while you sleep. Or fly-fish. Or go on a watercolour-painting course in Spain. Whatever you do, we're thinking of you.

5) You're on your own – part 1

All our lives it's been the same old story: "You can't do that". "If the opportunity is that good why isn't everyone doing it?" "I'm no expert but I wouldn't try it." "What if you get burnt?"

Both the authors of this book have witnessed naysayers at every turn. Doubting Cassandras who didn't want us to get ahead. People who were perhaps jealous of success, or were unhappy at the thought of being left behind.

These pessimists, these cynics, these churlish old maids have held others back too. We've seen it with our own eyes. Held their friends back from business ventures. Held their offspring in loveless marriages. Held the ambitions of their own partners firmly in check lest they stray too far from the plan, the beaten track, the nest.

Not us. It's tough striking out to do something new. The jackals, the sceptics, the bogeymen of success are ready to pounce. We've failed dozens of times of course. Our monumentally unsuccessful business ventures (not to mention botched relationships, investments and travels) include an ice-cream delivery service, an incense wholesale provider and a plan to induce oysters with marine pearls inside a tropical fish tank.

Can't you just see failure written into those commercial endeavours? One quite literally went up in flames.

But we persevered. We moved abroad to earn more money or improve our work-life balance. We gambled on property, relationships and laboured countless times for free with no guarantee of success. We've been lucky enough to be supported by like-minded people doing the same.

If we failed again at least we could sleep easy knowing that we'd tried. Better that than harbour a niggling doubt in our thirties, fifties, seventies or nineties about what if we had attempted something truly amazing. What if we'd grasped that glimmer of an opportunity in our twenties or forties or sixties or eighties? What if. What if?

And do you know what? A handful of the seeds we have sown, whether for us or our clients, grew into great trees. Some really big ones, like the giant redwoods in California that whisper majestically 100m (330ft) in the air. Those trees look like champions. Their success is unspoken.

We can rest a bit more nowadays. Take our feet of the gas. Drink wine. Not worry too much about money. Enjoy hearing our clients' happiness and success stories.

We can even spare the energy to write this book. It's nice to have the time.

We don't know where those doubting school friends, teachers and former bosses are today. We haven't kept in contact with the paper-clip counting colleague whose sole obsession was the bespoke office chair that his elevated status granted him.

When we have a fleeting reflective thought that elicits a twinge of malice towards those who tried to hold us back, we just open another bottle of rosé. After all, the best form of revenge is to live well.

Alas, those naysayers haven't been defeated. They still lurk in every society. East or West. Rich or poor. When you start any mission to change your life for the better you'll hear: "What if someone steals all your stuff?" "Are you not worried about paying all that extra tax?" "Does it not concern you that a complete stranger could copy your keys?" *

We've heard all those and more.

These doubters have their own reasons for holding you back, for sagging your success. Don't let them. Millions upon millions upon millions have done this journey before you. You're now one of them.

* To answer those three ridiculous doubts: 1) People don't book your property using an electronic paper trail that includes their cell phone and credit card details in order to burgle you. Paying guests prefer to visit your local museum or town centre instead. 2) Yes, if you make more money you might have to pay more tax. It's called getting a pay rise. We know of no-one who has refused a pay rise on the grounds that they have to pay a portion of their extra income in tax. 3) Anyone could copy your keys from the local window cleaner to a deranged local stalker. If this issue concerns you, invest in a digital lock instead.

6) You're on your own – part 2

There are some great resources our there to help you. Just Google 'should I use Instant Book' or 'what facilities do guests in a rental studio need' and the great Gods of the Internet will provide. Highly recommended websites include getpaidforyourpad.com and learnairbnb.com.

However, we think the feedback offered by the large rental portals like HomeAway and Airbnb is totally rubbish. Suckasaurus Rex.

To wit this 2017 marketing email from industry leader VRBO about "small changes to your listing (that) can help improve performance all year long".

1) "Upgrade your interiors with some minor updates. Your property's attractiveness is another major factor. Add a fresh coat of paint. Upgrade your TV to a flat screen." Thanks guys, what a screamingly obvious piece of 'advice' that was.

2) "Accept as many bookings as you can and minimize cancellations. Properties that accept bookings and cancel reservations only when necessary help us maintain high traveller satisfaction" Who'da thunk it?

3) "Respond as quickly as possible. When you respond to traveller requests and bookings within 24 hours, that creates a quality traveller experience." Noooooo. Seriously? You kidding me right?

4) "Get great reviews. Making sure you get a review from each and every guest will help you outpace your competition's reviews in the VRBO marketplace." Amazeballs.

Again, you're on your own. The multi-billion-dollar rental portals are not there to hold your hand. Find your own resources tailored to you. Hone your rental asset year-on-year. Beat the competition your way.

7) We're with you

We mean it. You're not really on your own. When we go to sleep tonight we'll be thinking of you. Heaven knows, we could even be staying in a rental space that you own. We'd be happy to pay you. After all, tens of millions of guests would.

What we're asking from you now isn't difficult. We don't need you to deliver a baby or learn Estonian in a week. You just need to follow the instructions in this book, plain and simple, then start making money.

You might be renting out a motor home. You might market your spare room like the Grover family whose lives were changed at the very start of this book. Whatever your property is, there will be cash tied up in it. We've just told you how to move that money to your bank account. Now it's time to watch the funds flow.

Ignore the cynics. Think of them only when you retire early or purchase your new car/boat/bicycle/education/guitar. If in doubt dip into this book again as necessary. Read the examples we've illustrated. Follow the experts' advice. If you have a friend or family member than wants to embark on your same revolution, then share it with them or buy them a copy.

Because this is a handbook to a revolution. Your revolution. There is cash in the attic my friend. Or in your spare room, or your holiday home or your garden shed. Or in your entire house while you head away on holiday this summer.

Make it yours. Today.

Chapter 16 written in stone

1) Airbnb has been around for less than 10 years and is already a household name. This market is worth many, many billions. It's time to siphon off your share.

2) Uber, Fiverr and all the other sharing economy companies are here to stay. Unless you want to try beating them, it might be best to join them.

3) More money usually translates as more freedom. We hope you become very free.

4) The opportunity is there for you to make money while sitting on the beach. It would be a crime not to.

5) Allegedly well meaning people will attempt to hold you back. They may be jealous, too timid to try themselves or simply cynical about life in general. You are not one of those people. You are a superstar. Enjoy the money that your new venture brings.

6) If you need any short term rental questions answered, Google it. Many millions have been in your position. The level of advice out there is unprecedented.

7) We're thinking of you. We've made this revolution before and in hindsight it was good fun, even if we spent more in Ikea than we first intended. The process is both simple and lucrative, which is why millions of others have also made this journey. Good luck on yours.

Printed in Great Britain
by Amazon